YOU TOO,

Can Be A

Happy Christian

by

BILL GEBROSKY

HARRISON HOUSE
P.O. Box 35035
Tulsa, Okla. 74135

All Scripture taken from King James Version of the Bible

ISBN 0-89274-030-2
Printed in United States of America
Copyright© 1976 Bill Gebrosky

II CORINTHIANS 5:17

Therefore if any man be in Christ, he is a new creature: old things are passed away; behold, all things are become new.

Credits

Mr. & Mrs. Ken LaRue   Mr. & Mrs. D. D. Regier

Jo Swearingen   H. Louise Rockhold

Helen G. Hutson

All poetry in this book —

*Inspirational Poetry for Daily Living—Bill Gebrosky
Acme Printing & Publishing, 1975, Wichita, Kan.

**Six Scriptural Steps to Salvation
Full Gospel Businessmen's Fellowship International

***Sinner's Prayer for Receiving the Saving Knowledge of Jesus Christ

Full Gospel Businessmen's Fellowship International

I Sought Him

I sought the Lord and He heard me,
    And He delivered me from all my fears.

I sought Him early in the morning,
    Now my mornings have turned into years,

How precious was the time of my seeking,
    Each moment, each hour of each day.

Oh, I'm so glad that I sought Him,
    The Life, the Truth, and the Way.

I wasn't long in my seeking,
    For you see He was seeking for me.

He saw me, another lost sinner,
    Who needed from sin to be free.

I'll never forget when He found me,
    The great look of love in His eye.

I remember the soul piercing question,
    When He said to me, "Why will you die?"

His look was one of compassion;
    His gaze was one of release,

But His touch was one of great mercy,
    For when He touched me, He gave me sweet peace.

Now I'm so glad that I sought Him,
    And I'm glad that He sought for me.

It's because of our searching and finding,
    That Christ's message shall flow out of me.

—Bill Gebrosky

Contents

1

The Long Search

He brought me up also out of an horrible pit, out of the miry clay, and set my feet upon a rock, and established my goings.

And he hath put a new song in my mouth, even praise unto our God: many shall see it, and fear, and shall trust in the Lord. Psalm 40:2-3

As of right now, class is dismissed! If you finish reading before I finish writing, feel free to go back to whatever you were doing!

But know this — I am positive that even though you may have many things that you could be doing right now, you have chosen instead to fellowship with me. I trust that through these written pages we can grow just a little bit closer to the Lord, and to one another.

For the first time, after nineteen and one-half years of being a Christian, I had decided to publicly give my story. Straight, without teaching, without preaching, without meddling, to tell it like it was without saying anything more than what the Lord has taught me about trusting Him.

I had some good news and some bad news for the people.

The good news was that I had received a *Scofield Version of the Bible* in the mail that day to replace the one I had lost several months earlier.

The bad news was that as I got out of the car to go into the meeting, I ripped a big hole in my pants! But my wife assured me that it didn't show: even if it did, I wouldn't have let it stop me from telling the people who were waiting to hear about the Lord and all that He has done for me.

My friends had requested that I give my testimony that night, and they were *both* sitting in the audience! The Master of Ceremonies for the evening got up and very lovingly began to introduce me. First, he read the first three verses of Psalm 111 and the first verse of Psalm 112. Then he started talking about how I was a man who was doing the Lord's commands and was happy in it, how my happiness was very contagious, and something about, "Like the words of the Psalmist, 'with this, Brother Bill can be a friend'."

With all due respect to him, you know something, Reader? I thought sure for a few minutes that I was attending a funeral, and that man was reading my *eulogy!*

It would be impossible for me to give all of my testimony. It takes hours just to talk about the blessings and the way the Lord has revealed Himself unto me. So, as I told that audience that night, all I can do is just start and when I find a stopping place I will stop.

I want you to see this testimony in the light of all He has done for me, how He has truly "brought me up also out of an horrible pit, out of the miry clay, and set my feet upon a rock, and established my goings. And he hath put a new song in my mouth, even praise unto our God: many shall see it, and fear, and shall trust in the Lord," because, Reader, that is exactly how it has been for me.

I want you to see my testimony as more than that. I want it to serve as your introduction to a great friend.

A friend is somebody who knows all about you and still likes you! A friend is somebody who has confidence in you when maybe no one else will.

If I have learned anything, I have learned that no matter what you do, no matter how much you try to run away, God is always there, wanting to reveal to you by His Spirit how much He loves you and cares about you. The Lord didn't give up on me even when I gave up on myself. He showed His great love for me by clothing me in my right mind in the psychiatric ward of a hospital while I was still unsaved, while I still refused to accept Him.

Through Christ I found myself. I began to know some of the beautiful things that I was capable of being and doing, but did not know were even possible until I surrendered myself to Him.

I grew up in the small coal mining town of Hardy, Kentucky, just a few miles from where the legendary feud between the Hatfields and the McCoys took place.

I have had the privilege of returning to Hardy several times in the past few years to speak in the Methodist Church, at what was called the "Full Gospel Old Timer's Meeting." The kids with whom I went to school and their families packed the church and the Lord poured out His Spirit upon all who attended. It was tremendous.

It was in Hardy, Kentucky, that I was introduced to alcohol when I was only six years old, by my father and the father of the pastor of the Methodist Church.

Little did my father realize that as a drink would be sown in a little child at the age of six, in seventeen years a hopeless alcoholic would be reaped. The Bible says, "Be not deceived; God is not mocked: for whatsoever a man soweth, that shall he also reap" (Galatians 6:7). But my father did not understand. When he dipped the cup into the barrel of homemade brew and held it to my lips to see me cringe at the taste, he thought that he was helping me to grow up to be a man, as he was a man in the only way he knew, the way he had been taught.

I got into a lot of trouble as a kid, at least now as I look back, I know it to be trouble. At the time, however, my buddies and I were just having a good time. We were called "wild" and "ornery" by some, and excused with, "Kids will be kids," by others. To fortify ourselves for our courageous escapades, I would break into my dad's wine cellar and steal his home brew. We kids picked the elderberries; Dad turned the berries into fermented wine; I would steal the wine; and the kids in the camp and I would drink it!

We would turn the railroad cars loose at the mine, ride them down the hill, and jump off in time to see the cars jump the track. We would turn cows loose in the schoolhouse on the weekend. You can imagine what a mess the teacher would find on Monday when she came to school! We would take the porch furniture belonging to the school teachers and the principal and see how high we could stack it on the smoke-stack of a steam shovel. We would break into the dynamite house to steal dynamite fuses, caps and dynamite, and go blow trees out from under opossum! — just little things to do for excitement.

I managed to graduate from the eighth grade, but the only person who failed to pass was a guy whose name was right below mine.

We moved to Pennsylvania in 1943. My mother and dad tried to talk me into staying in school but I figured an eighth grade education was all a man needed. Little did I realize that when I dropped out of school, I immediately entered into the "University of Hard Knocks," and I have not been able to drop out since! I am continually being educated each day.

I was asked to speak one time at Wichita University. Later, one of the professors came up to me and asked, "Mr. Gebrosky, how much education do you have?"

"How do you measure it?" I asked.

"What?"

"How do you measure it? If you want a pound of beans you get a scale!" I explained "If you want a yard of cloth you get a yardstick. Tell me how to measure my education and I will tell you how much I have!"

"What I mean is, how many degrees do you have?" he replied, eyeing me suspiciously.

"Oh, 98.6° and it has been known to go up to 103°!" I answered.

I figured that if he couldn't figure out how dumb I was, I wasn't going to be dumb enough to tell him!

Shortly before my sixteenth birthday, I lied about my age and signed up for the draft. My card arrived on my birthday. I went down to the Army recruiting office and enlisted in the Air Force. I forged my parents' signatures on the affidavit and it was accepted.

I was in the Army for ten months, stationed first at Fort Mead, Maryland, and then, at Kesslerfield, Mississippi. During that time I was AWOL (absent without leave) thirteen times. The last time I was picked up was for drunkenness, disorderly conduct, assault and battery, AWOL, and forgery. I was up for "court martial (trial)" when my parents found me and disclosed my true age. The dishonorable discharge proceedings were dropped, and I was given an honorable discharge, a GI Bill of Rights, $200.00 mustering-out pay, and told to go back to school.

I went back home — to Jeanette, Pennsylvania, but continued to "bum" around for a while. One day, I walked into a coffee shop for a snack. When the waitress came to bring me a glass of water and take my order, I thought to myself, "Say now, maybe she and I could have a few laughs together." When Naomi came back with my coffee, I asked her to sit down.

"How about going out with me tonight?" I asked, as I leaned back in my chair.

"I get off at nine o'clock," she told me.

"Okay," I said, "I'll come back and you up."

I went and had a few drinks and at nine o'clock I returned to the restaurant.

"Where are we going?" she asked.

"Let's go to the Amerization Club."

"I don't dance."

"That's okay," I said, undaunted. "We'll have a few drinks and I'll dance with somebody else!" I really didn't care, I just wanted to be with her.

"I don't drink," she said quickly.

"That's okay, I'll drink and dance with someone else." I remember my voice rising slightly and anger beginning to well up inside me.

"I don't go to those places."

I straightened up and looked her right in the eyes. "Let's go to the movies, then!" I demanded.

"I don't go to the movies either."

I exploded, "You don't drink, you don't dance, you don't go to the movies, what in the world do you do?"

"Well, I go to church once in a while; I go to Sunday school once in a while," she blurted out.

Her relationship with Christ was based upon do's and don'ts, but it isn't what we do or what we don't do that names us a Christian, it is what has been done for us — by Christ on Calvary. It is not by works of righteousness which we have done, but according to His mercy that He saved us. (Titus 3:5)

Jesus said, ". . . I have come that they (you) might have life and that they (you) might have it more abundantly" (John 10:10). There is not a person in the whole world worthy of God's salvation. *There is not a person who has been saved except by the unmerited grace of God.* Not one person is worthy of the fullness of the Holy Spirit, or of the blessings of the Lord, but because of the shed blood of Christ, He makes us worthy for the bountiful blessings of God.

When Naomi didn't do the things that I did, I dismissed her by saying in a cutting way, "Look, we have nothing in common. You may as well go home. I'm going out and get drunk." But you know, reader, in her *spiritual condition,* such as it was, she was better than any girl I had ever met in my life. I was never able to forget her. I guess I sensed that she must be something special.

Her brother came home from the Army, on furlough, and the family had a big dinner for him. Naomi was ashamed to even invite me to the dinner. She said she wasn't, but I knew that she was and we had a lover's quarrel.

Angry and frustrated, I decided to break her heart by joining the Navy, and we lost contact with each other. For two and one-half years I drank and fought my way half way around the world, striking out at everything and everybody. I went from *alcohol* to *goof balls* to *yellow jackets.* There wasn't a sin in this world that I didn't commit. I got transferred off the ship in Guantanimo Bay, Cuba.

I finally received a letter from Naomi and we began to correspond. I proposed to her in a letter but she wrote back, "Come home and we'll talk about it."

I came home and we became engaged. Returning to Cuba, I had an *itch around my heart* that I couldn't scratch. I asked her to marry me right away. This time she replied, "Let me know when you can come home again and I'll make the arrangements." I could hardly wait to get to the Commanding Officer to ask for another leave.

When I arrived in Pennsylvania, Naomi had a preacher *lined up*, a church *arranged for*, bridesmaids *standing by*, and all the paraphernalia you need for a church wedding. It was all set, and I didn't care how we got married, *"Just so we got it over with!"*, until my sister brought me up short by saying, "You know, Willie, if you marry that girl outside the Catholic Church, when you die you are not going to get the *'last rites'.'"*

Now, I was living like the devil himself but somewhere in the back of my mind I had an idea that I could live any way I wanted, because when I died the Priest was going to come along and water me down good and that would give me a chance in purgatory!

So, with *tongue in cheek* I went back to Naomi and said to her, "Look, I can't marry you by the preacher. You *gotta* marry me by the Priest."

"I ain't marrying you by no Priest," she said.

"Well, I ain't marrying you by no preacher!"

We argued for three days and finally decided on a compromise — we were married by the justice of the peace, and you know, we are still married today!

CHRIST AND I LOVE YOU

You may not think you're very much,
    and your life is not worth living.

You may not know how important you are,
    in the love that you have been giving.

You may not think you're anything,
    and no one cares for you.

You may think of yourself as a failure,
    in everything that you do.

But to me, you are very important,
    to me you're a bright morning star.

To me, you're a rose in God's garden,
    blooming right where you are.

To me, you're a kind gentle flower,
    so tender, so loving, so sweet.

To me, you're the kind of a person,
    I have always wanted to meet.

So don't live your life in the shadows,
    thinking you've failed in this life.

Remember that "CHRIST AND I LOVE YOU,"
    and He's chosen you for His wife.

Remember each day you're permitted,
    to live in God's lovely land,

As you hold out your one arm to Jesus,
    the other is holding my hand.

If you should turn loose of the Saviour,
    you and I both might fall.

So you are important to Jesus,
    but you're important to me, most of all.

2

The Lord Spoke To My Heart

For God sent not his Son into the world to condemn (judge) the world; but that the world through him might be saved." John 3:17

Ten months after Naomi and I were married, I was discharged from the Navy. In April of 1950, we moved to Wichita, Kansas, where I applied for a job at the Boeing Aircraft Company.

The director of personnel asked, "What are you skilled in? What training do you have?"

I had been a foot soldier in the Army and a torpedo man in the Navy; so, I told him, "Baseball."

"Baseball!" he exclaimed, "What position do you play?"

"I'm a pitcher."

To my surprise he said, "Well, you try out for the team. If you make the team you've got a job." So I went to work for Boeing Aircraft playing baseball!

Meanwhile, my wife's mother and dad, brothers and sisters all migrated to Kansas! It was a good thing, however, because I hadn't changed one bit inside. I was still mean and still believed that the priest could make it come out all right when it came time for my final rites. In fact, I got meaner, and the meaner I was to my wife the closer to the Lord it drove her. The closer to the Lord it drove her the more she prayed for me. The more she prayed for me the more under conviction I became and the meaner I got, and the meaner I got the more she would pray!

By this time a daughter had been born to us and 364 days later, a son. But, I left the care of my wife and kids up to her parents. I couldn't have cared less if the bills were paid, if my family had clothes to wear, or if they even had food to eat. I was only interested in my habit.

Finally, Naomi invited me to go to church with her. Mustering up her courage, she said, "Bill, you have never been in a Protestant church, how about going to church with us just one time?"

"Oh-h-h no!" I said emphatically, "I know about you people. If I go to church with you, you'll drag me down to the altar and you'll stomp me to death!"

"No," she said gently, "I promise. I promise that if you go, nobody will say a word to you."

"Okay then, I'll go," I agreed.

When Sunday came we all filed into the Central Assembly of God Church in Wichita. I sat on the very back row (I wanted to be as near the exit as possible!). You know something, when that preacher got up to preach, he preached on every sin I had ever committed! To make matters worse he kept pointing back there where I was sitting, telling me what a rotten, no good bum I was! I was convinced that my wife had written down all my sins and gave the paper to him with the admonition, "Okay we got him here; now the rest is up to you!"

If I hadn't been in that service that night, that poor preacher wouldn't have had a text! But, when he gave the altar call, not one person said a word to me. God, by His Spirit let me know that I was lost. He let me know that if I would go to the altar, like He was asking me to do, I would find joy. I would find the peace that I had been searching for, for a long time. I would not need stimulants in order to feel good. However, I thought my wife had *set me up for it;* so, I turned a deaf ear to the call. I refused to answer and left the church.

The whole episode reminds me of a man who went to church with his wife in much the same way as I had done, and the preacher preached at him the same way that I was preached at that night. The preacher kept pointing back at him telling him what a rotten, no good bum he was. He accused his wife of telling the minister all about him. He told her he would never go to church with her again. The very next service she went without him.

Moping around the house, he began berating himself. Here's this woman who washes his clothes for him, takes care of his kids, cooks his food, and a thousand other little things and he won't even do a simple thing like go to church with her. Finally, he said to himself, "I know what I'll do. I'll go down and I'll stand outside. That preacher won't know I am out there, and he won't be able to preach at me. He'll have to find somebody else to convict and you know, I can hardly wait to see who he picks out tonight!"

So, this man went down to the church, and as he stood there, outside the building, he began to realize that he couldn't hear too well.

Kicking at a loose board in the wall, he began to get an idea. If he crawled on his hands and knees under the church he would be under the platform. And that is what he did. He crawled to a spot directly under the podium. He thought to himself, "Man, this is tremendous! I am in the church house; I can hear the singing; I can hear the testimonies; I can hear the preaching, and the preacher don't know I'm out here! He can't possibly preach at me! Oh, I can't wait to find out who he is going to preach at tonight!"

The singing stopped and the preacher walked up behind the podium. "Friends," he said, "for my text tonight I have selected the topic, 'COME OUT OF YOUR HIDING PLACE'!"

Stamp! Stamp! Stamp! went his feet on the floor boards of the platform of that church as he emphasized every word!

I had made the blessed mistake of getting under the anointed ministry of the Word of God and I never was the same from that moment on. I went from bad to worse; and finally, I began to rationalize that the cause of all my trouble was my mother-in-law! I figured that if I would get rid of my mother-in-law, all my troubles would be over. My mind was that twisted and warped.

A plan began to form in my brain. I bought myself a 32-caliber revolver with the intention of killing my mother-in-law. The more I thought about it, the more it seemed logical to me to kill my wife, our children, and myself. When I came home that night, the gun was tucked under my belt. My wife was sitting in a chair, my mother-in-law was on the couch, and the kids were laying on the floor, coloring in coloring books. But you know, I could not bring that gun from beneath my belt. For fifteen minutes I stood there, glaring at my family until finally I turned around and walked out of the house.

They must have called the police and told them I was carrying a gun, because it wasn't too long before the police picked me up. They took the gun away from me, put me in the Cornado Hotel and told me to sober up. They told me that I could have my gun back the next morning. The next day I went back to the police station and claimed my pistol.

I took the gun home and threw it into a dresser drawer. While I was gone my wife dug it out and gave it to her mother who promptly hid it. It was never found until 1969, long after I had become a Christian. I said to her, "Hey, Mama, how about giving back my gun?"

"No," she said, "I am going to keep it until my dying day."

I said, "If you don't let me have it back, that may not be very long!"

Those four people are still living today. You know, if the Lord hadn't stopped me, I'd probably have shot them all. My mother-in-law and her husband are alive today and in their 80's!

After that I was the most miserable man who ever walked upon the face of the earth. I had drank away everything that I could beg, borrow, or steal. I owed every man and his brother; I was so in debt that it took me seven years after I became a Christian to pay back the indebtedness to all the people I had wronged.

I am happy to say, "When Christ came into my heart, He changed my life. I was able to make restitution, to my knowledge, to every person whom I had wronged before I became a Christian." One way it was brought about was with money, but I had to work to get the money!

I did not know what it was to lay my head on my pillow at night with a clear conscience. I was rotten and I knew it, but I couldn't seem to help myself. I didn't know how to help myself. I would not go to the place where people had tried to help me. I couldn't get to the place where people tried to get me to go, and that was to the one who created me, our Heavenly Father.

Finally, I received a letter from my mother. In it she wrote, "Son, if you ever get to the place where you don't know which way to turn, go see the Priest. He will tell you what to do to find peace."

Since I was at the place where I didn't know which way to turn, I went to St. Mary's Cathedral at Central and Broadway streets, in Wichita.

A priest came out and asked what he could do for me. With tears in my eyes I said, "Father, I am on my way to hell and I know it. Can you tell me what to do to find peace?"

I was like a little boy who was lost and a long way from home. I was searching for a kind policeman to take me by the hand and lead me gently to my Father's house. I trusted that priest because my mother had told me that that was where I could go to find my direction. But what I did not know was that people are only human, no matter who they set themselves up to be.

This man who was supposed to represent the Gospel was only a Catholic expounding the Catholic doctrine. He did not know Christ as his personal Saviour. If he had only known God's plan of salvation, he could have taken me to the sixth chapter of John where Jesus says, ". . . Him that cometh to me (for any reason) I will in no wise cast out" (John 6:37). He could have opened the Bible to the book of Romans and read, "That if thou shalt confess with thy mouth the Lord Jesus (Jesus is the Lord), and shalt believe in thine heart that God hath raised him from the dead, thou shalt be saved. For with the heart man believeth unto righteousness; and with the mouth confession is made unto salvation. For whosoever shall call upon the name of the Lord shall be saved" (Romans 10:9-10; 13). He could have taken me to Ephesians 2:8-9: "For by grace are ye saved through faith; and that not of yourselves: it is the gift of God: Not of works, lest any man should boast (that no man should glory).'' He could have read to me, "But as many as received him, to them gave he power (the right) to become the sons of God, even to them that believe on his name" (John 1:12).

Jesus said that He came not into the world to condemn the world, but that through Him the world might be saved (John 3:17). He said, "He that heareth my word, and believeth on him that sent me, hath everlasting life, and shall not come into condemnation (judgment); but is passed from death unto life" (John 5:24).

When you and I are in Christ Jesus we are not condemned, and when you and I are in Christ Jesus neither should we condemn one another.

But that priest didn't know how to lead me to Christ. He must have thought I was asking to join the church. He did the thing that he knew the best to do — he gave me a stack of Catechism books to read. He told me to take them home and come back when I had read them.

Lost and bewildered, I stumbled out of the church with the tears spilling over. I did not remember leaving the Parish house.

Later, my wife told me that when I came home, I ran through the house like a madman, into the bedroom, slamming the door behind me. When she pushed the door open, I was lying on the floor with blood squirting all over the place. I had taken a single-edged razor blade and slashed my wrists.

3

A Second Chance

Ye should shew forth the praises (excellencies of) him who hath called you out of darkness into his marvelous light. I Peter 2:9b

When I awoke I was in a strange place. I could not figure out where I was, nor did I know what had awakened me. With the smell of anesthetic and the sterility of the room, I guessed I was in a hospital. I had been admitted to the psychiatric ward of Wesley Hospital.

I tried to move, but both of my arms and my legs were strapped down. Far away as if down a long corridor or tunnel, I saw a man standing there whom I recognized as Rev. J. Boyd Wolverton. He had said something to me and now he was leaving.

Rev. Wolverton told me later that after I had been in the hospital for three weeks, he had come to see me. He looked into my eyes, but only saw a far away look. Knowing that I could not comprehend or understand anything he would say, he took me by the hand and prayed a short prayer for my healing.

What he did not know was when he said, "Amen," the Lord clothed me in my right mind! I saw Rev. Wolverton in my mind's eye when he left the room.

The doctor ordered thirteen electrical shock treatments and insulin shock treatments for me before I was released from the straps that held me down.

Next, I was transferred to a room with a roommate. My roommate must have invented the word "ugly." He was the ugliest person I have ever seen! He was baldheaded (I don't mean to imply that all baldheaded men are ugly!); there was not a single hair on his head. He had a disposition to match his ugliness. He didn't say, "Hello! How are you?" Nothing!

He just picked up his urinal and threw it at me, striking the wall over my head!

I ran out into the hall where the nurse asked me what was wrong. "That guy in there is crazy!" I exclaimed.

That incident was the confirmation of my healing, and a turning point for me. I was beginning my long road home, from the very lowest point that I could sink before entering the gates of hell.

A week later I was sent home. The doctors figured if I knew the difference between someone sane and someone crazy, I must be on the road to recovery.

The last week I was in the hospital I was made a "trustee" over some of my fellow patients. One day I was asked to take two of the men to the park for some fresh air, rest, and relaxation. We sat down on a bench in the park — one man on one end of the bench, the other man on the other end, and I sat in the middle. All of a sudden the fellow on my left began motioning with his hands. He clamped his knees together, threaded an imaginary something in the air, grasped it with both hands, and flipped it over his back. In a few seconds he leaned back, pulled real hard, and started winding like crazy! When he finished, he would start the pantomime all over again. Soon the man on my right started doing the same thing. I just sat there and watched. I was one of them, you know, so I understood them.

It wasn't long before a "cop" came up and said to me, "What on earth are you guys doing?"

'Sh-h-h!" I answered him. "Be quiet, those guys are fishing!"

"FISHING!?! Man, this is a park. There is no water around here. You'd better get these guys out of here!"

"Okay," I said, as I picked up my own imaginary pole, reeled it in and handed the guy a fish! (That last part isn't true, but wouldn't it have made a great ending?)

After I was released from the hospital, I decided to leave Kansas and return to Pennsylvania. I stayed there for two years.

One day in September of 1954, I received a letter from my father-in-law.

"Bill," the letter read, "if you will come back to Kansas, Boeing Aircraft Company said that they would give you your old job back."

I had just been laid off the job where I worked in a brewery.

I want to tell you, a brewery is the last place for an alcoholic to be working! When most people were having "coffee breaks" we were having "beer breaks"! Every time I went home I would have to crawl over the hill.

The offer from my father-in-law sounded good and I decided to return to Kansas. My father-in-law, however, was waiting for me. He had salvation on his mind, and he wasn't going to mince words over it. The first thing he said to me was, "How about going to church with me?"

"Okay." I agreed so quickly that I even surprised myself.

The service had already begun when we arrived. I never told Brother Wolverton, but I never forgot the look on his face when I walked into that church! He *set his glasses* and took a second look to see if he was really seeing who he thought he was seeing. I don't know who he had been preaching at during the time I was gone, but he sure looked excited when he saw me walk through that door! I guess, at that time, I must have been *good preacher's bait!* Anyway, Brother preached and again the Lord by His Spirit dealt with my heart, but I still refused to answer the altar call to give my life to Christ.

I was the most foul-mouthed individual anyone ever talked to. Every day on the job, the men would gather around me for a dirty story the way you would for coffee and doughnuts.

On October 3, 1954, I came home from a glorious church service and sat down to watch a football game. Lighting a cigarette, I began to let the message of the morning penetrate into my subconscious mind. Suddenly, the *truth of the gospel of the Lord Jesus Christ came home like a glorious penetrating light.* It just seemed as though the Heavenly Father was saying to me, "BILL, I LOVE YOU."

I didn't have a friend. Those who did love me had long since disowned me. My wife was close to walking out on me. My own mother and father had told her she was crazy if she lived with me another day. No one really thought I was worth caring about; so, those four words, "Bill, I love you," had great meaning and struck the very core of my being.

There — in my living room with the television set blaring — the Spirit of the Lord spoke to my heart. He just reached down and took a 200-pound weight off my shoulders. I took the cigarette I was smoking out of my mouth and put it in the ashtray. I threw the package of cigarettes that I had in my pocket at my uncle. Surprised, he asked, "What's wrong with you?"

"I've got religion!" I said.

"What?"

"I got religion!"

My wife came running into the room, followed close behind by my mother-in-law. "What's the matter?" they demanded.

"I've got religion!" I repeated, "and I can't wait to get to church tonight!"

Before I knew what was going on, they were on the phone calling all our relatives who had backslidden. They told them to come to church that night because God was going to do something!

When I went to church that night, and the preacher got up to preach, no longer was the Word of God like a sword cutting the innermost part of my soul. It was like milk to a new born babe's heart. Peter said, ". . . desire the sincere milk of the word, that ye may grow thereby" (I Peter 2:2).

I was being fed that night for the first time, and when they gave the altar call, I got up and went to the altar to make an outward confession of an inward work.

When my relatives saw that the Lord was down to saving the "Pollocks" they thought the Rapture of the Church was soon to take place! They all came running down to the altar! Revival broke out in our church!

I went to work the next day, dressed the same, but walking differently, and inside an entirely different man.

"Coffee break time" came and the men began to gather around me for their daily quota of dirty stories.

"Gebrosky! What kind of story you got for us today?"

"I'm a Christian," I said. Two or three of them looked at me with a funny look on their faces; another man spewed out his coffee, and another looked — expectantly waiting for the punch line. Finally someone said, "WHAT?"

"I got saved yesterday."

"You did what?" By now, everyone was listening and a few were beginning to snicker.

One fellow pointed his finger at me and said, "Let me tell you something, Gebrosky, you are so rotten that even God wouldn't have anything to do with you!"

"Men," I replied, "I only know one thing. Last night was the first night that I ever laid my head on the pillow with a clear conscience. I slept like the new born babe that I was."

I hadn't been able to sleep because of all the troubles and problems that I had. The Lord gave me peace that no one has been able to take from me in twenty years. The peace, not that the world gives, but that He gives. The assurance that if He loved me when I knew nothing about him, how much more He must love me with each passing day. He introduced Himself to me by His Spirit. He gave me joy I have never lost.

All day long the men smirked and teased as they cat-called to me, "Hey, Deacon!" I didn't even know what a deacon was. I thought the reason they called me "Deacon" was because Vernon Law used to pitch for the Pittsburgh Pirates and they called him "Deacon Law!" I thought they called me "Deacon" because I was a ballplayer!

The teasing didn't bother me, however. My mind was on more important matters. I was thinking about going to church again that night, and I could hardly wait. I wasn't disappointed; the service that night was tremendous.

After the service was over the Pastor asked me if I had a Bible. When I said, "No," he placed one in my hands and insisted that I read it. He told me to read it as a love-letter to me from God. Reader, that is the best advice that I can give you, if you are willing to listen to me. "Read your Bible as if it is a love-letter to you from God."

4

How To Make A Covenant With God

*Ask, and it shall be given you; seek, and ye shall find;
knock, and it shall be opened unto you: Matthew 7:7*

I had changed all right; I was different, but the world
had not changed around me. Becoming a Christian, feeling
the Lord's love, and reading His love-letter to me each day
did not take away my circumstances.

When I went to work the boss gave me the dirtiest jobs;
the men ridiculed me, laughed at me, teased me, and taunted
me. I would come home dead tired and with my *ego* rubbed
sore; but, walking into the house did not assure me that there
I could escape the world either. The wife nagged me, and the
kids were bawling.

I said, "I quit! I'm not going to church any more. I have
gone and been faithful and it hasn't seemed to make any
difference."

I don't know what I expected, but I suppose that I
thought if the Lord loved me, He would treat me like a king
and make everything nice for me. I didn't quite understand
fully that Jesus, in dying on the cross for me and everyone
else, had already done just that, with the assurance that
". . . greater is he that is in you, than he that is in the world:"
(I John 4:4). That we are to be strong in the grace that is
in Christ Jesus. "And the things that thou has heard of me
among many witnesses, the same commit thou to faithful
men, who shall be able to teach others also. Thou therefore
endure hardness as a good soldier of Jesus Christ. Therefore
I endure all things for the elect's sakes, that they may also
obtain the salvation which is in Christ Jesus with eternal
glory" (II Timothy 2:2-3; 10). You see, I will still a babe;
I had not yet grown up in the Lord.

No sooner had the words, "I quit," come out of my mouth, than the same still, small voice within, which had said, "Bill, I love you," told me, "you are going to give account for your own soul." Paul tells us, "So then every one of us shall give account of himself to God" (Romans 14:12).

Know this, reader, we are individuals whom God has called personally. "Are not five sparrows sold for two farthings, and not one of them is forgotten before God? But even the very hairs of your head are all numbered. Fear not therefore: ye are of more value than many sparrows" (Luke 12:6-7). We cannot blame anyone else for our circumstances. We can't say, "If she would quit nagging me, I wouldn't . . ." or "if the boss would treat me with a little more fairness, I would . . .". How you live and react to the circumstances of the world is your responsibility to God. No person should be able to rob you or me of our joy in the Lord.

The Apostle Paul assures us that absolutely nothing but ourselves can separate us from the love that is in Christ Jesus. "For I am persuaded, that neither death, nor life, nor angels, nor principalities, nor powers, nor things present, nor things to come, nor height, nor depth, nor any other creature, shall be able to separate us from the love of God, which is in Christ Jesus our Lord" (Romans 8:38-39).

"And the Lord, he it is that doth go before thee; he will be with thee, he will not fail thee, neither forsake thee: fear not, neither be dismayed" (Deuteronomy 31:8). Our Father does not want us to fail. He wants to reveal Himself unto us. He wants us to know that He does love us and we can trust Him in all things. His Word says, "It is better to trust in the Lord than to put confidence in man" (Psalm 118:8).

I went to church on my third day of rebirth. I didn't know anything about the Holy Spirit, but that night I received the baptism in the Holy Spirit. The Lord endued me with power from on high and from that day to this I have not been ashamed of the gospel of the Lord Jesus Christ. "For I am not ashamed of the gospel of Christ: for it is the power of God unto salvation to everyone that believeth; to the Jew first, and also to the Greek" (Romans 1:16).

The fourth day, I went to work and was assigned another dirty job working on an airplane. As I worked I began to think about what my Lord had done for me. I thought about His crucifixion on the cross, on that hill called "Calvary", just outside the walls of Jerusalem. I began to realize that every drop of blood that Christ shed on Calvary was a drop of His love for you and me.

Wiping my hands on my coveralls, I took a pencil and a piece of paper from my pocket. On that grimy piece of paper, I began to write the first song I had ever written in my life. I am going to quote just a few of the words for you. I called it "RED DROPS OF LOVE."

"My life was vile and vulgar, it was so wrapped in sin,

My heart was cold and heavy, there was no peace within,

I knew no joy or happiness, 'till I looked above,

And then I saw coming down to me, red drops of
    His love.

I praise the Lord for this great love, and the peace that
    I have within.

I thank Him for the drops of blood that cleansed my
    soul from sin.

I thank Him for His blessed son who died upon the tree,

And shed the red drops of His love just for you and me.

I know the Lord is with me, for His Spirit dwells within.

I know the Lord has cleansed my heart, and saved my
    soul from sin.

So, I will tell the sin-sick world of Christ's redeeming
    blood,

And how He paid the price for me, with the
'RED DROPS OF HIS LOVE'."

When I finished those words, I stood there crying like the babe that I was, not really caring whether anyone saw me.

A short time later, Brother Wolverton asked me if I would speak at the Union Rescue Mission. My first reaction was to back off from him and cry defensively, "Pastor, if you want me to fold bulletins, if you want me to paint the church, if you want me to cut the grass — anything, anything that you want me to do with my hands, I'll do it, but don't ask me to speak. I am no speaker. I have no education. *I don't know nothin' about nothin'.* I just won't do it because I can't do it!"

He just stood there *toe-to-toe* with me and didn't move one inch. "Don't tell me 'no'," he said. "Go pray about it. After you have prayed about it, if you can tell me 'no', I'll accept it."

I went home and into my bedroom to tell the Lord how ridiculous the whole idea was. He couldn't possibly expect a clod like me to preach the Gospel. That was what I thought I was going to do, but it didn't turn out that way. Instead, when I dropped to my knees, I entered into a covenant with God.

I want to emphasize the fact that you can make a covenant with God. But, I ask you this, "Before you ever make a covenant with God, be sure that you are willing to do what you agree to do."

To make a covenant with God, take a piece of paper and write up at the top:

"EVERYTHING I WANT GOD TO DO FOR ME."

At the bottom of the page write down: "EVERYTHING I WILL DO FOR GOD."

That, my friend, makes the contract legal. It is good for Him, it is good for you. It has to be good for both parties. You tell God what you want Him to do, and put down what you are willing to do. I guarantee you on the authority of the Word of God, that He will do everything that you ask Him to do, but be sure you will do what you tell Him you will do. "For which of you, intending to build a tower, sitteth not down first, and counteth the cost, whether he have sufficient to finish it" (Luke 14:28).

To my knowledge, I haven't put any amendments of my own on my out and out contract that I made with God twenty years ago. I have not broken that contract even though it cost me my business; it almost cost me my home; it cost me a lot of friends; it cost me a tremendous amount of things external, but it HAS NOT COST ME MY JOY. It has not cost me my peace; it has not cost me my happiness because I have kept the contract with my Lord. "And ye now therefore have sorrow: but I will see you again, and your heart shall rejoice, and your joy no man taketh from you" (John 16:22).

This is the contract or covenant that I made on my knees many years ago:

"God, you know I am not a speaker.
You know that I do not know anything.
But, if you will give me a message tonight,
that I can stand in front of those people and
speak, and confirm it with some sign, I will
never ask for an invitation to speak.
I will take every invitation that I receive as
coming from you, knowing that you have prepared
the hearts of the people, and that you prepared
my heart with the Word to be taken to them.
                                        Amen."

I got up off of my knees with a sense of great peace. I had placed the whole matter of my speaking *publicly* in the hands of the Lord. It was up to Him now to let me know what it was that He would have me do.

I went down to the Union Rescue Mission, knowing that that might be the first and last time I would ever stand *in public* to speak, and a man named C. W. Brown went with me. He not only went with me and witnessed the first message I ever preached, we also sang together that night, for the first time. Later we went together several times to speak and deliver a message in song.

But, when I stood up to speak at that mission, my mind, at first, was blank. The only thing I saw was miserable drunks and derelicts scattered about that room. Then, without warning, a *scroll appeared before me in my mind's eye.* The Lord gave me my first sermon. He had told me what He wanted to do. He was upholding His part of the contract. The scroll kept unrolling and I couldn't read it fast enough.

But, I had also asked for a sign to confirm that this was from the Lord. The sign came, too, in the form of a drunk who staggered down the aisle and asked me if it was true that God would do for him what He had done for me. He came in answer to the altar call that C. W. Brown had prompted me to offer, because I had not thought about offering an invitation to others. I hadn't grown to the point of looking out for my brother. I was like a newly-wed still on his honeymoon, the bride whose eyes stayed on the bridegroom with wonder and love that such joy was possible.

That drunk dropped to his knees; we stepped down, and began to pray for him. We only prayed for thirty seconds, when the man stood up, glowing like an electric light bulb; he was stone sober!

There was no doubt about it being the sign I had asked for, the confirmation that God had agreed to the covenant. From that day to this, I have never had to ask for an invitation to speak. In the last twenty years (at this writing), I have averaged over two hundred and fifty messages a year! I have crisscrossed the United States and have been in Hawaii several times, because God has never broken His contract and I have never broken mine.

Our Father wants to do things for us. He wants to give to us. He wants us to be happy. When we don't let God give unto us we rob Him of a blessing. But the hardest thing for us to learn is how to receive.

I have dappled in many businesses without compromising my contract with God. I was in the insurance business. I would carry out my business and also fulfill my contract. I would travel around the country where people would offer me an offering for coming and teaching them the Word of God. I would say, "No, thank you. You give it to your Pastor. Give it to a missionary."

And do you know? I was going around the country convinced that I was the kindest, most generous speaker those people ever met!

The truth was, I had too much pride to receive an offering. I was too proud to let Him give me something. I had myself convinced that I was just a big, benevolent Pollock going around the country with a generous heart.

During the course of all this, the man with whom I was in business broke me. He welshed on a contract which cost me thousands of dollars and left me thousands of dollars in debt.

The first thing I did was to go to my banker who knew about the situation.

"I don't have any money," I said. "I'm broke. I don't have a job. I don't know when I can pay you."

If you owe your banker any money, go tell him. You might be surprised how he'll work with you. For seven months I never made a payment to the bank. But all during that time I couldn't understand why God had permitted this to happen to me. My contract had five years to run. It had brought me in $21,000 that year. I had it all figured out in my mind. I could live on $7,500 a year, and invest the balance of the $21,000. I would take the offerings I would receive and I could preach the gospel for fifteen to twenty years! That's a great way for a fellow to figure it out, right?

Within ten days of the day I made that commitment, I was broke. I had nothing coming in, I had no job, I had no income. I owned some property across the street and as a last ditch effort to stay afloat I said to the Lord, "If it is your will for me to go into full time evangelistic work at this time, let me sell my house across the street. It's got to be sold in twenty days." Then, I took off for the golf course!

When I don't know what to do, I do that which I enjoy doing the most — I go golfing. During those twenty days my wife worried enough for both of us. I figured there was no sense both of us getting ulcers; so I went out and played golf!

5

Dead Poodles And A Renewed Commitment

For whosoever will save his life shall lose it: and whosoever will lose his life for my sake shall find it. For what is a man profited, if he shall gain the whole World, and lose (forfeit) his own soul (life). Matthew 16:25-26a.

I am still a great story teller! I didn't give that up when I became a Christian; I just tell a different kind of story now. The stories I tell now are more like *Aesop's Fables* in that they usually contain a moral.

I would like to share a story with you about a woman who had a lovely poodle. It was a beautiful poodle. She put a little pink ribbon around its neck and bathed it until its white fur glistened.

That poodle would stand up, stick its tongue out, and dance around the room. It was truly a lovely thing.

Everybody liked the lady's poodle, but one day it died. However, the woman couldn't bring herself to bury the poodle; so, she took that poor thing, wrapped it in a beautiful blanket, and set it in a cupboard.

I went to see her one day and knocked on the door. I said, "Hello, young lady, how are you doing?"

"Oh, pretty good," she replied. "Come in and let me show you my poodle."

Well, it was about a week old, you know, and it had begun to smell quite a bit. I said hastily, "Oh, I'm sorry, you know I-I forgot, I-have-an-appointment. I-I gotta go. Good-bye!" and I left.

About a month later I decided to go back and see her again, thinking that surely by this time she had come to her senses. I knocked on the door and again she answered.

"Come on in," she invited. "Let me show you my poodle."

By this time you can guess how *rotten it had gotten!* I said, *"Oh, Madam, I gotta go!"*

Three months later I thought surely she would know that she should have buried it by now! I went back, and knocked on the door again, "Well, how are you getting along?" I asked.

"Okay," she said, "Say, let me show you my poodle."

I never went back to that house again! It wasn't that I didn't like her; it was because I just wasn't interested in her stinking poodle.

Now comes the moral: when you have something in the past that should be buried, bury it! People are not interested in your poodle! Every time they come into your presence and ask, "How are you getting along?" they don't want to hear, "Well, just fine but let me tell you what *so* and *so* did to me . . ." If you do, they will leave you and you may not understand why they leave so quickly. They don't leave in a hurry because they don't like you. It is because they can't stand your stinking poodle! If you keep on bringing out that rotten poodle, people aren't going to come back!

This is what I did; I played golf and I told everyone I saw about my beautiful poodle that had died. I told everybody and his brother about how I was wronged. During those twenty days that I waited for my house to sell, I golfed every day, except Sunday. I took six strokes off my game! It really came down. Also, during that time I was offered seventeen jobs. The last job that was offered to me was with the First National Investment Company. It was three days before my "fleece" ran out when a representative of the company offered me $400 a week plus commissions to start. That's a pretty good job to start with, so, I told the man, "I'll tell you what I'll do. I'll let you know in three days."

"You will let me know in three days?" he said, incredulously. "Listen, the only reason we called you is because we heard you are a man who knows how to make decisions!"

"Fine, I just made one," I told him. "I'll let you know in three days."

"Listen, Gebrosky, we are going to fill this position. You go ahead and call us; we *might* talk to you."

Three days passed; the house didn't sell. I never went back and talked to the man. I decided to start an insurance business of my own. I called it the "College Hill Insurance Agency." My home address is 255 North Holyoke in Wichita, Kansas. We have an apartment in the basement. I went to the city officials and asked them to address the apartment 3211 East Second . . . that way I had two addresses to put on my business cards. I didn't want anybody to know that I was working out of my home.

So, I started my insurance agency, but I needed $3,500 for operating capital. I couldn't go to my bank and ask for it; they may have loaned it to me, but I was afraid to go to them. I went golfing instead! While on the fairway, I told the Lord, "I need $3,500."

On Monday a man came to my house and gave me a $1,500 check! He explained, "When you get on your feet, you can pay me back."

The following Thursday, my father sent me a check for $500. The following Tuesday, a man came to my house, he was very cocky and laughing. I steeled myself for anything — except the amazing thing that did happen!

"Hey, Gebrosky!" he began.

"Yeah?"

"What is this I hear about you losing your business?"

"That's right."

"I suppose you learned your lesson. You are going to quit trusting people, aren't you?"

"No," I said, honestly. "I am going to continue to trust people. I am going to continue to lose money."

"You know, I figured you were that kind of a guy. Here, here is $1,500. Will that help you?"

There was every last dollar of the $3,500 I needed!

I hung up my golf clubs and started developing the College Hill Insurance Agency! I worked it for ten months, paid back the indebtedness to the people from whom I had borrowed the money, and supported my family. At the end of that time, I sold my business for $7,500, and went into the evangelistic business, as a layman, driving a Lincoln Continental.

People, when you are driving a Lincoln Continental and wearing a good suit, preaching a positive gospel, the people don't think you need any money — and they don't give you any!

Because of that, I had to go back to work. I worked in many businesses, and every business I have worked *in*, the Lord has permitted me to be a success.

The truth of the matter, however, was that I was a frustrated businessman. My mind and heart were never on the business. I have only worked about 20 per cent of the time in any business I have ever been in, since I got out of the insurance business. I was only interested in carrying the gospel, and the Lord has provided the means with which to do it.

I have been asked to "fill-in" for some notable speakers. One time Henry Krause (now with the Lord), who was at that time the international director of the Full Gospel Business Men's Fellowship for the state of Kansas, was scheduled to speak in Kansas City. It was to be a big evening, with Henry Krause giving the message, and the Singing Duey's supplying the special music.

The auditorium was packed; everyone was waiting for Henry Krause. But at the last minute he couldn't come, and I was asked to take his place.

Can you imagine, all those people expecting a dynamic speaker, and all they got was a dumb Pollock!?

I tried to explain to the audience, when I saw the disappointed looks on their faces, the definition of a "substitute." I said, "If you knock a window (glass) out of your building, you have to get a piece of cardboard to replace it until you can replace the glass."

After the meeting some dear old lady came up to me and

said, "Oh, Brother Bill! You are not a substitute — YOU ARE A REAL PANE!"

Was she trying to tell me something?

I had many opportunities in my business, but as I told you I was a frustrated businessman. Finally in December of 1972, I decided I was going to quit this traveling around the country, preaching the gospel, struggling, worrying about where the money to pay our expenses was going to come from. I decided I was going to work and send somebody else.

That month of December, I cleared $10,000 in 30 days! I said, "Lord, you are so good to me. You are right behind what I am going to do. I am going to concentrate on my business while I send somebody else to carry your gospel."

He said, "I didn't do that for you. The devil offered me the world, and you are willing to sell out for $10,000 a month?" . . . "Again, the devil taketh him up into an exceeding high mountain, and sheweth him all the kingdoms of the world, and the glory of them; and saith unto him, All these things will I give thee, if thou wilt fall down and worship me" (Matthew 4:8-9).

"All right, then," I answered. "I'll never work another day, but the first time one of my creditors calls and asks where his payment is, I'll take it as your sign for me to quit 'preachin'' and go back to 'workin'!"

Since that day (and as of this printing), I have not worked, except in the gospel. I have been able to give my thoughts to the gospel, to minister to the needs of the people.

After my talk with the Lord, a banker came to my house on December 23, offering me a position in an insurance business — a tremendous position. He had a partner and they were buying an agency. I was told I would be given a third of it. I would have a salary plus expenses.

I wanted to accept it, but while that man was talking to me, my Father spoke quietly to my heart: "Bill, if you were training your son to take over your business, and when you got ready to turn part of it over to him, he decided to go into another business, *how would you feel?*"

"Sir," I said to the man, "I can't accept the position."

"You can't accept?" His mouth dropped open and he stood there with a surprised look on his face, because he knew I didn't have any other opportunities or deals.

"That's right, I can't."

"But why?"

"I just can't."

I turned the opportunity down, believing that the Lord will not tell us anything by His Spirit that He doesn't show us in His Word. He must confirm it in His Word.

A short time later as I sat reading my Bible, the Lord directed my attention to the 21st chapter of John. Jesus had appeared twice to the disciples after His resurrection. Peter told John and the other disciples, "I'm going fishing." The disciples replied, "Wait, we will go with you."

They fished all night and didn't catch a thing. The next morning as they were coming into shore, they saw Jesus standing there.

"Children, have you any meat?" He asked. What He was saying was, *"Have you ett yet!?"*

The disciples explained to Jesus how they had fished all night and caught nothing.

"Cast your net on the right side," He instructed the men.

Now Peter could have said, "Lord, the fish don't know the difference between left and right. The boats have been drifting all night. We know these waters by heart." But, *because the Lord told them* to cast their nets, they went back out onto the water and cast their nets over again, as they had been instructed.

Amazingly, the nets began to fill and they couldn't pull them in for all the fish . . . 153 fish, as it says in the Gospel of John. It was not *"Charlie Tuna;"* it was tuna that tasted real good! It was the *"choice fish of the sea."* I don't believe the Lord put any *culls* in that net. I think He sent the choice fish of the sea for those disciples! However, when they came to the shore, Jesus had fish already cooking on the fire. He also had bread on the fire. He did not take any of the disciples fish!

Reader, Jesus doesn't need your fish. A lot of us think, "Boy, if the Lord doesn't get my money, He isn't going to make it!" He doesn't need your money. He doesn't need your bread. He doesn't need your substance.

What He needs is YOU. Once He has you, everything you have belongs to Him. He did not take one fish out of the disciples' net. He had His own fish on the fire along with the bread.

Jesus turned to Peter and asked, "Peter, lovest thou me?"

"You know all things, Lord," Peter replied. "You know I love you."

"Feed my lambs."

"Peter," He repeated, "Do you love me more than this?"

"Lord, I told you, you know everything. You know I love you!"

"Feed my sheep," Jesus said and He asked Peter one more time, "Peter do you love me more than all of this?"

Peter answered Him, "Lord, you know what? You get on my nerves! You know everything, you know I love you."

"Then, feed my sheep."

You see, Peter did not love the Lord at that moment. He did not know the meaning of the word *"love"* until after Pentecost.

When a man comes home from work and his wife says to him, "Do you love me?" and he says to her, "Are you kidding? Who do you think I'm working 40 hours a week for? Who do you think I'm out there slaving over those machines for? Who do you think I'm bringing that money home to?"

That isn't what she wants to hear. She doesn't want to hear what her husband is doing. She wants to hear a simple, "Yes, Honey, I love you."

That's what the Lord wants to hear. He didn't want to hear Peter's resume of what he thought he was doing for

Jesus. All Jesus wanted to hear was, "Yes, Lord, I love you."

When a man asks his wife, "Do you love me?" What do you think he wants to hear? Do you think he wants his wife to say, "What do you mean? Why do you think I have been taking care of these snotty-nosed kids for? Whose house do you think I'm keeping? Do you think I wash your dirty old clothes because I like to?"

That's not what he wants to hear. All he wants is a simple, "Yes, I love you."

That is what the Lord wants to hear. That is what the Lord wanted Peter to say.

There comes a time in your life (and mine) when you can stand and sing, "O, how I love Jesus," all you want to. You can stand and raise your hands and say, "Lord, I love you," all you want to, but if you really want to know how much you love the Lord — come to me and ask me — and I'll tell you just how much you love Him.

If you really want to know how much you love the Lord, go ask your neighbor, and the neighbor will tell you how much you love the Lord; because, you see, my friend, the only way you and I will know that we love God is by the love we have for each other. He said, "By this shall all men know that ye are my disciples, if ye have love one to another" (John 13:35). If you want to know how much you love God, go ask your black brother. If you want to know how much you love God, go ask someone who is beside you. If you want to know how much you love God, ask someone and they will tell you. If you want to know how much you love your husband, ask him. He is the recipient of any love that you are showing. Only he is qualified to tell you how capable you are of loving him.

These were some of the questions I had to ask myself. When I was faced with the decision of accepting that position, I had to (unconsciously) ask myself as the Lord spoke to me by His Spirit, "How much do I love God?" With my answer, He confirmed what I had agreed to, in complete trust, that my Lord would not forsake me nor leave me. I had *renewed my commitment* to Him.

I could go on and on talking about the blessings, talking about the good things. But, Reader, this Christian life is not an easy life. I have had my mountains and I have had my valleys. Frequently, I ask myself why I couldn't have stayed home just as easily . . . why I can't be a passive Christian. You know, it takes no effort to be nothing. A person can be nothing with no effort at all.

I can sit right down in my easy chair and never speak another word from now until Jesus comes. Would you say I was a righteous man? Would you say, "Oh, what a holy man he is! I never heard him say a word about anybody, never saw him wrong anybody. He doesn't do anything!"

My friend, doing nothing is the greatest sin a man can ever commit. I do a lot, and I make a tremendous amount of mistakes, but I forgive myself for every one of them; because, I am going to make some more mistakes tomorrow. The only thing is, I refuse to worry about all the mistakes I am going to make tomorrow; because, if I begin to worry about them and *die tonight,* and not have a chance to make them, it would be a waste of time spent in worrying, don't you agree? So, I'm going to go right on making mistakes today and enjoy making them. I intend to learn from those mistakes, and I don't intend to miss that opportunity! Today is all the time you really have.

I have a friend, I'm sure he won't mind my sharing this with you, who called me one day and invited me to lunch. "The doctor told me that I have to have open-heart surgery," he said to me. "Would you have lunch with me so we can talk?"

We sat there at the lunch table talking about the things of the Lord. We shared the blessings of the Lord together, on the top floor of the Holiday Inn.

Later, he and I went to his office where we had the privilege of praying together. This friend was my banker and I want you to know, it is a tremendous blessing to have a banker with whom you can pray, a banker who will counsel you and encourage you, one you know will pray with you when you are talking about your needs.

I was convinced as my name is "Gebrosky" that when we finished praying Clayton would not have to have his surgery. In fact, I told him so before I left his office. He went into the hospital trusting in the Lord, but not really knowing the outcome. The doctor had told him, "You may live ten days; you may live twenty days; you may live a year, or you may live twenty years." You see, doctors have to be safe. After the first ten days you are on the plus side!

Clayton only stayed in that hospital three days and is still alive today! I believe the reason for that is because the Father loves him, that the Father is concerned about him, that the Father has many places to take him as a testimony that HE could not and will not bring any of us so far and then let us fail.

Our Father brings us to a place where He can reveal Himself to us, where He can let us know that He loves us, that He is concerned about us.

What's happening in your life today is for your good. Whatever the Father is permitting to happen right now is for your good, and whatever is happening at this moment in my life is for my own good. It is His permissive will, He is permitting it. But, He promises us He will not let us be tempted above what we are able to stand. "There hath no temptation taken you but such as is common to man: but God is faithful, who will not suffer you to be tempted above that ye are able; but will with the temptation also make a way to escape, that ye may be able to bear it" (I Corinthians 10:13).

As long as we are upon this earth, we shall have mountains and valleys. Without the deep valley, there cannot be beautiful mountains. Without the battle, there cannot be the victory. But know this, when you climb your last mountain, the Lord will take you home, and not until.

So rejoice! Today may be your last mountain to climb.

And you'll be so happy that you followed my way,
   with just one more mountain to climb.

ONE MORE MOUNTAIN TO CLIMB*

As I travel down this road of life
　　through mountains and valleys I find

That heartaches and happiness go hand in hand,
　　when you have one more mountain to climb.

I trip and I stumble as I'm starting my climb,
　　with the rocks and the brush in my way;

The moment I feel that I just can't go on,
　　a still small voice seems to say:

"Come, I'll go with you. I'm one step ahead.
　　Just look to me and you'll find

The road is not easy that you're called to take;
　　you have one more mountain to climb."

So, climb this small mountain that I've placed in your way;
　　it won't be long 'till you're standing on top.

Then, look about, all my beauty to see; then you'll
　　know why you must not stop.

For millions are dying in the valleys below,
　　As you go to the valleys you'll shine;

The people will look at your face, all aglow
　　and long for your mountain to climb.

Yes, you are the one who will take Me to them,
　　and you'll be my voice and my feet,

But I am the One who'll deliver from sin,
　　for I am the one they will meet.

Many will follow when you mention my name,
　　the halt, the sick, and the blind.

And you'll be so happy that you followed my way,
　　with just one more mountain to climb.

6

In The Joy Of The Lord

I know thy works: behold, I have set before thee an open door, and no man can shut it: for thou hast a little strength, and hast kept my word, and hast not denied my name. Revelation 3:8

I rededicated myself to the Lord and vowed that I would always try to listen for the still, small voice. It would always be "not my will, but thy will be done," believing completely that all things work together for good to them who love God. (Romans 8:28)

I also developed my own philosophy. I decided that I wasn't going to argue with anyone who didn't believe as I did. I decided that everyone can believe what they want to believe. If we all make it to heaven, we will have a great time, but if you go to hell, I "ain't" going to get excited. I "ain't" going to miss you!

When I was in Hawaii, I called a man and we talked for a while. He asked me to call him again when I got back to the States (or to the mainland). I agreed, but when I arrived home, I kept putting it off until finally when I did remember, I had put it off one day too long. He had had a little indigestion on Wednesday night and he went home and went to bed. At two o'clock in the morning, he couldn't breathe, and by three o'clock he was dead.

Reader, there can be only a heartbeat between you or me and eternity. You never know when you are going to go, but I will tell you this, you can know where you are going. If you die right now and you don't know that you are going to heaven, then you are going to hell, because God's responsibility is to reveal to you and me which way we should take. The choice is ours.

There is not a person who knows my faults like I do. I know *me*, inside and out. I have been trying for a long

time to always be honest with myself. I know I have weak-
nesses. I know I have faults. I know that I make many mistakes, but I know that if I keep right there, grinding in the
mud, I will get out of that mistake on to a smooth highway,
only to make another mistake and get into the mud again.
Remember this, as long as we are going forward, we will
never have to worry about going backward.

The Apostle John writes, ". . . These things saith he
that is holy, he that is true, he that hath the key of David,
he that openeth and no man shutteth; and shutteth, and no
man openeth; I know thy works: behold, I have set before
thee an open door, and no man can shut it: for thou hast a
little strength, and hast kept my word, and hast not denied
my name" (Revelation 3:7-8).

When I went to Hawaii to speak at the Full Gospel
meeting there, the leaders for the event forgot to coordinate
it, and they had two speakers lined up. Consequently, I was
cancelled out, and that was good for expenses! But, the
Lord opened meetings that were far more important than the
ones already set forth. He closed the doors on some and
opened them on another.

The Lord has command of the winds and the Bible tells
us many times of His power over the wind. Jesus rebuked the
wind and it was still. (Luke 8:24) Psalm 147:18 tells us,
"He sendeth out his word and melteth them: he causeth his
wind to blow, and the waters flow." David the Psalmist
relates how great God is. "Who layeth the beams of his
chambers in the waters: who maketh the clouds his chariot:
who walketh upon the wings of the wind" (Psalm 104:3).
We also read, "The voice of the Lord is powerful; the voice
of the Lord is full of majesty . . . The voice of the Lord
shaketh the wilderness. . . ." (Psalm 29:4, 8). When Paul
and Silas were in prison there suddenly was a great earth-
quake; so that the foundations of the prison were shaken,
and immediately all the doors were opened, and everyone's
bands were loosed. (Acts 16:26)

Reader, know this, God has control over all the doors
in our lives. He can shut doors that are open to us that
would lead us astray. He can open doors that are shut against
us which would prevent us from going where He would have
us to go. He is all powerful and His power reigneth supreme.

No man has enough power to restrain God from what He sets out to do. When He opens a door for us, no man can shut it. God has bestowed many honors upon me since I became a Christian.

Gideon was a town clown. (Judges, Chapters 6 and 7) The Lord said to Gideon, "I'm going to make a general out of you," and Gideon replied, "Me, Lord? I'm just a town clown. I don't know too much about anything. People laugh at me. People say all manner of things about me."

But, the Lord said, "Gideon, I want you to take 300 men with bugles blaring, with lanterns burning bright, and you are going to put 120,000 of the enemy to flight."

Gideon answered, "Lord, Me?"

He said, "Yes, you." And do you know Gideon learned something. He learned that *with the Lord* he was a *great general,* but without Him he was just the *town clown.*

Through that lesson of Gideon, the Lord taught me a lesson. He told me, "Bill, with me you are going to do great things, but without me you are just *another dumb Pollock!*"

Today I know that anything I am or ever hope to be, I owe all to Christ. I know that through these many years, in spite of all my faults, my failures, and my mistakes, the Lord has permitted me to see things and to go places. When I was in the insurance business, I lost all my business, lost all my money, lost all that the bank could loan me, but in the process, through their patience and understanding, my credit is still "Triple A." That's the trouble. I can borrow it too quickly! It's the paying back that gives me problems. However, through it all, the Lord met my every need. He taught me a great lesson — to trust Him. I had to trust Him because I had no one else to turn to, and through that I learned that the Lord didn't bring me this far to fail. He brought me here to teach me something.

One time I was scheduled for surgery. I had been hacking and spitting for ten months and thought it was just a head cold. I found that after I got back from a meeting my doctor and my wife had gotten together and had me pre-admitted to the hospital. I refused to go unless they promised to let me out the next Thursday. I had to be out of the hospital by then, because I had to leave for Hawaii the next day.

Under those conditions I was admitted to the hospital. I underwent all kinds of tests, and they found that I had a head full of infection.

During my stay in the hospital many things happened. I had the opportunity of counseling with more than 15 people. The floor on which I stayed was called the "floor of no return." You either went to the graveyard from there or a miracle took place! I didn't know it, so I was happy while I was there!

The doctors would come in and examine me and ask how I felt. I told them it was embarrassing because I felt so good. I felt too good to be sick! Two people died on that floor the first night I was there.

The next day, a lady called and said, "Mr. Gebrosky, I was told that you are on the same floor as I am, and if you would come down and pray for me, the Lord will heal me."

"I am in my pajamas," I said.

"That's okay," she told me, "come on down."

I went out to the nurse and said, "If anybody is looking for me, I'll be down in room 792."

"What are you going to do down there?" she asked.

"I'm going to pray for that lady's healing."

"Gebrosky, you've got to be the craziest patient we've ever had on this floor!"

The lady in Room 792 attended a meeting later (where I was asked to speak). I had to apologize to her because I didn't recognize her. She looked so different. I asked her at the meeting, "Won't you come up here and testify? I added, 'Ladies and gentlemen, here is a lady who was prayed for by a man in his pajamas'!"

She came to the microphone and said, "I just want to briefly state what has happened. For five years I have had ulcerative colitis and I have been under the care of approximately ten different doctors and just recently I spent ten weeks in St. Francis Hospital. Your prayers, Brother Bill, helped me a lot. I am living on my own now, praising the Lord, and getting better every day. I gained five pounds, and for me that is a lot of pounds!"

I know she won't mind my saying this. When I walked into her room in the hospital, she was being fed intravenously. She was lying on her back; her eyes were so sunk in her head that it broke my heart, but I didn't want her to see how I felt. I counseled with her about Christ, shared with her some of the poems the Lord has given me, and when we finished, we prayed for her. Her eyes, her sockets, filled with tears. The next day before I left, I went back to see her again. She was sitting on the edge of the bed, feeding herself. Not much, but feeding herself.

I know I was in that hospital not only for the purpose of the lady who called me, but also to lead the men who were in the room with me to a saving knowledge of Jesus Christ.

When I had the money I didn't have the time to go places. When I went broke, I began to go everywhere! When I left the hospital, I went to Hawaii, where I had been invited to come, "on faith." When people say to you, "Will you come on faith?" what they mean is, "Will you come at your own expense and take what you can get in offerings while you are here?"

I went, "on faith!" and the Lord moved in such a beautiful way that we were invited back for a little over three weeks. I have gone back (at this printing) a couple of times since then.

The first time I went to Hawaii, we ministered in many different meetings: a Catholic church — three times; an Episcopal church twice; in prayer meetings, Bible studies; and Full Gospel Businessmen's Banquets. *Wherever we went we saw that the Lord would never let a Pollock make a liar out of Him!*

He will do exactly what He said He would do — meet the needs of the people. Jesus said, ". . . I am the way, the truth, and the life: no man cometh unto the Father, but by me" (John 14:6).

On a Thursday, I spoke in Mauai, Hawaii, in St. Ann's Catholic Church. A woman came forward for prayer. She said that her doctor was going to put her on a kidney machine. The next Sunday morning, she came to the Methodist Church (where I was ministering), carrying a bottle of kidney stones. She had one stone in that bottle which was long with jagged edges. She witnessed to me that she had passed that stone with no pain and no blood.

On Friday night, I spoke in Father Winkler's Church of the Good Shepherd Episcopal Church. On Saturday, I spoke for the Women Aglow. On Saturday night, I spoke for a banquet. Then, after speaking in the Methodist Church on Sunday, I flew to Honolulu that night to speak at the Grace Bible Church.

When we arrived at Grace Bible Church, a lady with terminal cancer and another lady with heart trouble came forward for prayer. Three weeks later as I prepared to leave, those ladies testified that the doctor had given both of them a clean bill of health. Praise the Lord!

During my second visit to Hawaii, a lady at a prayer meeting asked me if I would pray that she could get to Kona where I was going to minister. She said, "I got a brother; I got a husband; I got several relatives over there I would like to bring to the meeting." I didn't know at that time that the meeting had been cancelled. I flew on to the big island of Hawaii, and held a city wide meeting in the high school building. It was tremendous to see God by His Spirit and grace bring the young people to a saving knowledge of Jesus Christ.

When I found that I was cancelled out, on Monday and Tuesday in Kona, the chapter president said, "Bill, come over for a Saturday morning breakfast." I agreed and spoke for a breakfast in a home that Saturday morning. While I was there, the lady (with whom I had prayed concerning the meeting and her relatives) called and asked me about the Monday and Tuesday meetings.

"Where are the meetings going to be held?" she asked.

"Well, I think they have been cancelled, but wait a minute and I'll ask the chapter president."

I said to him, "Hey, there is a lady on the phone who wants to know about the meetings on Monday and Tuesday. Is it definitely cancelled?"

"Ask her how many people she can bring," he said.

"She says that she can only bring 25."

"Twenty-five! Boy, if she can bring twenty-five, we've got a meeting!"

The meeting was *on* again, in Kona. But first the lady invited us to meet in her home.

When I arrived on Monday, 12 people were seated in the living room. I felt like Peter going to the house of Cornelius.

As I began to talk about Jesus, tears started flowing down their cheeks. Several different races were represented: Japanese, Oriental, Korean, Japanese-Hawaiian. We all talked together about Jesus. I had no intention of giving an altar call that morning, however, the Spirit led me to say, "All those who would like Christ to become the center of their lives, please stand to your feet." Ten people out of the group stood up and we joined hands. We prayed the sinner's prayer together.* We then returned to our seats to talk about what it means to be a new babe in Christ Jesus. As we were talking, the Lord told me, "Pray for that woman." She was a Japanese-Hawaiian. Turning to her, I said suddenly, "Young lady, do you mind sitting in that chair? I'd like to pray for you."

As I prayed for her, the Lord healed her. She stood to her feet, raised her hands and shouted, "Now, Jesus, I believe! I have seen a miracle!"

Unknown to me that lady had to be helped into that apartment. She had undergone a hysterectomy, a nervous breakdown, and quite a few mental problems, but the Lord so moved upon her, filled her heart with such joy that it astounded the kids as they saw her running up and down the slopes, in and out of the condominium and the parking lot! Needless to say Tuesday night they all came, and we had two great nights in the Lord.

I came back to the mainland and went to West Virginia where the pastor and I scheduled a baptismal service. We were going to baptize ten people: four Catholics, two Baptists, and four Methodists. If you have ever been wading in

*The sinner's prayer given on page 127.

a creek in West Virginia in the early Spring, you know it's cold! When I waded into that water it was so cold the pastor had baptized three people before I got my breath.

There was a young lady who stepped into the water and as we were talking to her (before we even touched her), she bowed like a fish in the water and out. She was baptized with a power that we had nothing to do with! When she came out of that water, her long hair flung the water. She glowed like a neon sign!

I received this letter from a lady in Ninole, Hawaii. It reads: "Remember me? I am the one you met in St. Peter's Church in Ninole. I want you to know that I am in good health. In fact, we are all in good health. Almost every time I am free from work, I read the Holy Bible with interest, with love, and with understanding. I know we will see one another once more. Now, when I do my school work, it comes easily. I ask Jesus to help me and He does. My heart is aching. On the outside of me I am happy laughing and all joyful, but inside me, I am so sad. I want so much to learn about God, to become a better child of God.

Thank God I met you for you opened my eyes to many things, Brother Gebrosky. If there is any free time, could you please teach me another of God's messages? Take care, as God fills you with His love and wisdom to teach all.
                Sister Rosemarie Gomez, Ninole, Hawaii

While in Hawaii I had the privilege of staying in a quarter of a million dollar home. I'm not used to staying in places like that! It was the most beautiful home I had ever seen. There were about 80 or 90 people gathered there to worship the Lord. Many things happened in the lives of those who attended, but one thing in particular was a Methodist schoolteacher who came forward and said, "Brother Gebrosky, I just have to have the Holy Ghost!" We counseled with her for just a minute, and we started to lay hands on her and pray, but when we touched her, she hit the floor. When she hit the floor, her head snapped and when it snapped, she began speaking in tongues.

I went on to pray for the needs of the others. After about five or ten minutes I looked over and she was sitting up. "I got it! I got it!" she cried in rapid fire — like a machine gun taking off, and away she went!

She came with her husband to the Full Gospel Businessmen's Meeting on Saturday. At the close of the service, her husband came up and said, "Mr. Gebrosky, I don't know what has happened to my wife. When she came home from the meeting she was like a new bride. We haven't been happier in our lives. I have a piece of property in Honolulu, and if you will come to Hawaii and teach what you have been teaching since you have been here, I will give you that property and help you put a building on it." It was a tremendous honor, and I told him so, but I can't go, and yet, I would like to go.

While in Hawaii, I was taken deep sea fishing one day when I had a few hours of free time. After days of speaking two and three times a day, I needed the rest. We sailed 20 miles out of Honolulu and for two hours caught nothing. A man by the name of Solono was with me. He said, "Bill, come up here on the bridge, and let's have a prayer meeting." I went up and we started praying by ourselves. Solono suggested that I pray that we catch some fish. There were five people on the chartered boat, and I didn't want to be selfish, so I prayed that the Lord let us catch five fish, one for each person. We had no sooner said, "Amen," than all five poles started singing!

We had five fish on five poles at the same time! Have you ever tried to bring in five fish at the same time? The one closest had to bring in his fish first; the rest of us had to play ours and wait our turn. We no sooner reeled those fish in when the lines began to sing again. When we finished fishing, we had 91 fish: 15 dolphins, 75 tuna, and one Hawaiian salmon. Right there was the "proof of the puddin!" I took a picture and have it as evidence.

This is not a fish story! It is a true story! As we sailed back toward shore, the three men who had not prayed with us went to the captain. "Boy," they said, "Captain, you sure know where the fish are!"

"Don't give me credit for that," he told them. "These two guys held a prayer meeting and the Lord sent the fish to the boat!"

That is exactly what the Lord does. When the Lord said, "Peter cast your net on the other side," and Peter pulled in the fish, his nets couldn't contain all the fish! And you know what kind of fish he caught? He caught the best! Do you think the Lord was going to let him have a bunch of *clones?* That is why Peter was so free with his money. (Acts 2:45)

After Pentecost, Peter went broke. That's right! After Peter received the Holy Ghost, he went broke. When he and John went up together into the temple at the ninth hour, the hour of prayer, they met a man who had been lame from birth. Peter said to him, "Silver and gold have I none; but such as I have give I thee: In the name of Jesus Christ of Nazareth rise up and walk" (Acts 3:6).

He took the man by the hand and lifted him up. Immediately, the bones in that man's feet and ankles received strength and he began leaping and shouting and praising the Lord! (Acts 3:7-8)

There are those who would call the man to task, and say, "I don't think you should do that."

Reader, the people who won't leap and shout and praise the Lord are those who don't have any reason to do it! Can you imagine that guy at the temple saying (when he was asked what happened), "Oh, I was sitting here minding my own business and the Lord stuck His nose in my business. I didn't want to be healed! I wanted money. Now, I gotta go to work . . . no more welfare for me!"

I received a tape from a man, named "Danny-O," in Hawaii. He invited me to come to speak in October of that year. He was with the underworld. He was dealing in vice, prostitution, and dope, when he found Christ. He went to the mafia boss of the islands of Hawaii and said, "I am a Christian and I want to get out of the racket."

"Okay, Danny," he was told, "since you are a Christian, and you won't indulge in these vices any more, we won't bother you. But, if you interfere in the racket, your life won't be worth a plug nickel!'

I have received several tapes from Danny-O, and I have laughed and cried over what the Lord is doing in Danny-O's and others' lives. When they took me to the airport to send me back to the "mainland," they put enough flowers around my neck that if I had an undertaker, I could have gone to heaven! They are just wonderful people. In the middle of the International Airport, they said, "Men, gather around and let us pray for our brother before we send him home." I was a little nervous because they were a little loud. There in the middle of that airport terminal, they gathered around me. They all laid hands on me (one hand touching me, and one hand raised to the Lord), praying for me!

I thought to myself, "Whew! I'm glad that's over!" Then they moved in closer to me and said, "Now, Ladies, you come and pray for him!"

I received this letter from a 90-year-old man.

"Dear Brother Gebrosky,

I'm still here. Many years ago these words gave me great comfort. A very dear brother of mine lost his right arm caused by an accident. The intern at the hospital asked me to witness the operation.

I held his left hand as we waited for his recovery. He became conscious. He looked at me saying, 'Do I still have my arm?' The scene was too much for me and I lost control. Then, he became convinced he had lost his arm. He looked at me again and said, 'Don't be sad, BD, I'm still here.' The lady in white put her arms around me and said, 'Yes, you should be glad your brother is still here.'

Since that day, ladies in white have had a fine influence over me. Today I realize that I have lost more than half of my vision, and more than 60 per cent of my hearing, as well as the greatest friend a man can ever have, a devoted wife, and with her — went my home. Deep losses have slowed me down and caused me many lonely days, as well as sleepless nights.

Today, I thank God for so many dear friends who are helping me to live. It is a great and glorious experience having you with us today. May our heavenly Father reward you greatly for being here. I am glad to be here with you. Love you all? I say I do. I am so glad to be here.

Sincerely yours,

BD Cook"

This 90-year-old man's daughter came to see me and asked, "Will you please come to Kailua, Hawaii, and talk to my father? He is afraid to die." Ninety years old and he was afraid to die!

When I went into her home she had beautiful paintings all over her house, about 30 or 40 of them. She was an artist. She took me into her father's room, and we began to talk about the things of the Lord. I discovered that he used to live in Wichita, Kansas, many years ago — long before I was born. We talked about Wichita, how it had changed. As we talked, the Lord made the opportunity to talk to him about Jesus and about His love, about the things that had transpired in his life, and how God loved him. We began praying and the tears flowed down that man's cheeks. He said he was not afraid any more.

As I left the house, the daughter asked, "Do you like my paintings?"

"Oh, yes," I said, "they are beautiful."

"You can have any one you want," she told me.

I looked on the wall and there was a painting about six feet long and about four feet high. It was the most beautiful ocean scene I had ever seen. It just looked like the rocks and reefs where I was sitting one day listening to the song, "We Are Children of the Lord." When I looked at that painting, it was so beautiful that I was afraid to ask for it. Instead, I chose another one called "Akaka Falls." She boxed it up and gave it to me.

The moment she handed the box to me, the Lord taught me another great lesson. He said, "Bill, that is the trouble I have been having with you for 18 years. I have offered you the best, but you have settled for second best."

From that day on, I vowed, "Lord, I am always looking for the best, no longer will I settle for second best with you."

I have another letter to share with you. This one is from Fairmont, West Virginia:

"Dear Mr. Gebrosky,

I want to thank you for praying for me at the Jesus Outreach in Fairmont, West Virginia. My arm had been hurting me for over a month. I was afraid it might be my heart because I also had shortness of breath. I haven't written sooner because I wanted to see if my healing was complete. Every day I would think my arm was going to hurt. Praise God when He does anything it is always complete!

I thank God for you and your ministry. Pray that you will continue bringing glory to His name!

Sincerely,"

I am sharing these letters with you just to let you know that many have been praying for me and the Lord's ministry, and I, and those with me, have received many blessings from those prayers. The Lord has taken us many places. What a long way he has taken me since that night at the Union Rescue Mission! And I want you to know when we all enter into heaven we will all go in together, because you will share, and I will share in that which God is using all of us to glorify His name.

I know that I am just a child and I know that I am not a speaker. But I know that with the Lord, I can be all things to all men, that I might win some to Christ.

In verse 11 of the 34th Psalm, the Lord says to us, "Come ye children, hearken unto me: I will teach you the fear of God."

When the Lord meets your need, He is not going to ask for it back. He says He wants us to take the need He is going to meet today and give it away.

If you are sick, my friend, come to Him, He will heal you so that when you see someone else who is sick you can pray for them and see them healed the way you were healed. If your marriage is on the rocks, He will mend your marriage; then, when you find somebody who is having trouble you can be used to mend their marriage for Him. If you are having a financial need, He is going to meet your need financially. Likewise when you find somebody with a financial need, He is going to meet their need.

If you are lonely and have heartaches, He is going to be a friend that is closer than a brother. When you see somebody who is lonely and has heartaches and sorrows, you are going to be a friend to that person and He is going to answer his or her need because you asked Him.

There won't be any strings attached. It will not be based on that person for whom you prayed. It is going to be based on HIM and HIS love for YOU.

Have you ever felt that your life wasn't worth living? Have you ever thought nobody ever really cared for you? Have you said to yourself, "Man, what's the use? I have been trying for 20 years and I seem to be in the same old rut. Nobody cares about me. Nobody is concerned." My friend, that is known as self-pity. I know because I have been there.

Bartimaeus, the blind beggar, heard that Jesus was passing by. He reached out to him and cried, "Jesus, thou son of David, have mercy on me."

Jesus said, "Bring him to me."

The blind man was brought before Jesus. Jesus said to him, "Bartimaeus, what would thou that I should do for thee?"

"Lord, I am a blind beggar," Bartimaeus answered, "I want to receive my sight."

Jesus told him, "The faith that caused you to come to me is the faith that is going to make you whole." (Mark 10:46-52)

I ask you, "What is your need?" Do you want to be filled with the Holy Ghost? Do you want to be healed? What is your need at this very moment, this very hour? I ask you to let God who has authored your faith bring you to the place where He can meet your need.

The faith that would bring you out of where you are, to where you can receive that which Jesus has to offer, is the faith that is going to make you whole, because you are coming in Jesus' name.

What is your need? I cannot personally be there in your home to pray with you, but through these printed pages and through His Spirit, I pray this prayer for you.

Our heavenly Father, we do praise thee and thank thee for thy love for us. We thank you, Lord, for this moment that you have brought us to; for the heartaches and sorrows and sicknesses of thy people. We praise you for that, Lord, because we know that through this need you are going to manifest yourself. You are going to reveal yourself unto us, so that, Father, you will be glorified, that Christ will be lifted up. Now, Father, I ask that at this moment, you who are the author and the finisher of our faith, to speak to every heart and every life. Give each person the confidence and the assurance of knowing that you have heard their heart's cry and you are going to meet their need. We thank you for it, Father, for we receive your many blessings.

In Jesus' Name,

Amen.

7

Heavenly Places

So then Faith cometh by hearing, and hearing by the word of God. Romans 10:17

MY FIVE HOURS IN HEAVENLY PLACES—

On March 2, 1976, while I was playing golf at the Clapp Golf Course in Wichita, Kansas, I started walking up the 12th fairway when a very sharp vice-like grip began squeezing all of the air out of my lungs. The pain was in the middle of my chest.

I stopped at once and began to gasp for air. It was several minutes before I got enough air to continue. I never dreamed of having a heart attack.

I finished the 18 holes with a lot of discomfort, and I left the golf course and drove down town to the post office to see if I had received any mail.

When I started out of the post office, I passed out for just a few minutes. The past hour had been one filled with pain and shortness of breath.

I drove to my home about thirty blocks away, took the golf clubs out of the car and carried them up the steps to our utility room. By this time my heart was beating a mile a minute, and I couldn't get my breath.

My daughter, Jill, met me at the door. "Dad! What's wrong with you?" she asked.

I said, "Call your mother, I think I am having a heart attack."

We jumped back into my car and drove to Wesley Hospital in Wichita and entered the emergency room. I was examined; they placed a glycerin tablet under my tongue, called my doctor, and had me admitted to the intensive care unit of the hospital. This was around five o'clock, Tuesday evening, March 2.

The following Sunday I was supposed to be in Reevesville, West Virginia, to start a revival for the Methodist Church where Rev. Bill Preston was the pastor. When Dr. Drevetts, my doctor, came in, he told me to cancel the meetings; I wouldn't be going anywhere for at least ten days, or more.

As I looked at the monitor that was registering my heartbeats, I wondered what the erratic beats of my heart meant. Dr. Drevetts had instructed the doctors and nurses to answer any question that I would ask. So, I asked one of the doctors what was the meaning of the sharp line that shot up every so often on the monitor. He said very softly that if the line wasn't gone by morning, I might be.

Not once did I ever think to pray for myself. Not once was I afraid. I was in perfect peace at all times. The only remorse I felt was for the fact that I might not get to go to West Virginia to minister to those wonderful people there.

I learned some tremendous truths. For one, I learned that faith is not something that you work up, nor do you pray it down. ". . . faith cometh by hearing, and hearing by the word of God" (Romans 10:17). FAITH is something that is. If the Word of God is in our hearts, then we are living in faith. So, faith is ever present with us as we continue to walk according to the Word of God.

While I was in the hospital I had the opportunity to talk to more than 28 people concerning the hope that I had in this life and the life that is to come after death. The nurse who was assigned to take care of me, along with the staff, sat at the foot of my bed with tears flowing down their cheeks as we talked about the wonderful love of Jesus.

From ten o'clock on Tuesday evening until three o'clock Wednesday morning was the most glorious time of my life. I know now what the Apostle Paul meant when he said, "I don't know which is best, for me to go and be with the Lord, or stay and be here with you, but for your sakes I'll stay."

I was in the presence of the Lord. The only way I can explain it is like this: take the most beautiful moment of your life and multiply it with as many numbers as you can, and that will give you an idea of what the atmosphere of Heaven is like.

Paul said, "that eye hath not seen, nor ear heard what the Lord has prepared for those who love Him, but it has been revealed to us by His Spirit, for His Spirit searcheth all things, yea the deep things of God. (I Corinthians 2:9-10)

During those five hours I was aware of the decision I was making, whether to go and be with the Lord or stay. Now that I know that I will not miss Heaven, I decided to stay and lead as many people as I can to the wonderful place that is prepared for us.

At three o'clock in the morning, I was still wide awake. They gave me medicine to make me sleep, but it didn't faze me. My heart was still beating out of control, so I decided to write the thoughts of my heart.

I pressed the button on my bed, and I raised up to a sitting position. Then, I wrote the following poem:

REFLECTIONS

If today would be the last day, that
I could spend upon this earth;
I would evaluate my yesterdays and what
they were worth . . .
I would think of all the people who have
walked into my life . . .
I would ask myself this question, "Did they
find joy, or was it strife . . .
Will they be glad they met me, or are they
happy to see me go?"
Am I the kind of person they were glad
they got to know?
Did I set a good example of our Christ's
redeeming love?
Will they want to follow me, to His mansion
up above,
Or when my name is spoken, will they shrug
and say, "Oh well,"
If that man has gone to Heaven,
I'll just spend my life in Hell.

When I finished the poem I started to lie down. The nurse said that before my head hit the pillow I was asleep. At that moment my heart slowed down and has been all right ever since.

Two days later I was released from the hospital with no restrictions.

While I was in the intermediate unit where I had been moved from the intensive care ward, something wonderful happened. About three years ago, in Fairview, West Virginia, a young lady came to the meetings where I was speaking. When she found that I lived in Wichita, she said her mother and father lived there also and asked me if I would "look them up." I said I would, but for three years I was unsuccessful in finding them. They moved me into a room where there was an elderly man in the bed next to mine. A man and woman were visiting the man. When the nurse hooked up my "electrodes," a friend of mine came in and said, "Bill Gebrosky, you're the last man I thought would ever be in the hospital."

When he mentioned my name, the couple stood up and asked me if I knew a man by the name of John Green in West Virginia. I said I did, and then they asked me if I knew Brenda and Larry Cummins. When I told them I knew them, the couple said that they were Brenda's parents, and the man in the bed next to mine was her grandfather! Isn't the Lord good to all of us? He will go to any extreme to get His children together!

I did leave the hospital in just three days. Praise the Lord for His sweet wonderful presence in my life! God reveals Himself unto us! "But as it is written, Eye hath not seen, nor ear heard, neither have entered into the heart of man, the things which God hath prepared for them that love him. But God hath revealed them unto us by his Spirit: for the Spirit searcheth all things, yea, the deep things of God" (I Corinthians 2:9-10).

THE KINGDOM AS OPPOSED TO THE KINGDOM OF GOD—

> *But seek ye first the kingdom of God, and his right-eousness; and all these things shall be added unto you.*
> Matthew 6:33

I believe there are two groups of people in the world today — those who are on their way to Heaven and those who are on their way to Hell.

In "Christdom," I believe there are also two groups of people on their way to Heaven — those who have found the *kingdom of God,* and those who are on their way to the *kingdom of Heaven but have missed the kingdom of God.* The *kingdom of Heaven is a place where we are going when we leave this earth. The kingdom of God is where we can be while we are on this earth.*

I would like to deal with the kingdom of God at this time, and explain what I think it is, where I think it is, whether we can get there, and what we can expect after we arrive.

While Jesus was on this earth, His disciples asked Him to teach them how to pray; so, Jesus instructed them to pray, "Our Father which art in heaven. . . ." (Matthew 6:9). He was telling them to pray to our Father who is out somewhere. Our sun is 93,000,000, miles away and is one and one-half million times larger than our earth; so, Jesus couldn't have told them to ask the Father to send the heavens down here. Jesus continued His prayer, "hallowed be thy name, *thy kingdom come* . . ." What was He saying to His followers? He was saying to pray that the King of Kings would reveal unto them the kingdom that God the Father wants to dwell in.

Where is the kingdom of God?

If I told you that I had diamonds buried in my back yard, and that if you would just come and dig, you could have all that you find, wouldn't it be your place to dig if you wanted to be rich?

The Lord sent Moses to lead the children of Israel out of Egypt and take them to the promised land. They were *God's chosen people;* they were in bondage and God wanted them to be free in the land of promise. You and I have been bought with a price, the blood of Jesus. We are God's *blood-bought* people. He wants to take us out of our bondage to a life of freedom. When we get to heaven we will not need any help. *It is here and now that we need to know what God has for us.*

The Bible is filled with promises, over 500 to be exact. *It is God's promised land for you* and me while we are on our way to heaven. The *promises are like diamonds.* They are *hidden in the Bible.* We must dig for them. Every promise you find in the Word of God is yours. Find it, apply it to your life. The results of the promise will make your life shine for Christ as diamonds shine in the eyes of men. The kingdom of God is the Word of God; those who are abiding in the Word are living in God's kingdom. The Holy Spirit is the one who makes the Word of God come alive to us. And it makes our loving Father very happy when you and I seek to follow His Word.

Jesus says that wherever you are, the kingdom of God is. (Luke 17:21) The Spirit of the Lord dwells in us — not only to set up residence there but to be president of our lives.

Jesus tells us, "Therefore take no thought, saying, What shall we eat? or, What shall we drink? or, Wherewithal shall we be clothed? (For all these things do the Gentiles seek:) for your heavenly Father knoweth that ye have need of these things. But seek ye first the kingdom of God, and his righteousness; and all these things shall be added unto you" (Matthew 6:31-33).

Many men and women today are seeking the material things of life, for in them they think they will find happiness. Jesus said in Luke 12:15, ". . . a man's life does not consist in the abundance of things he possesseth." So, I added, "his life consists in those things which possesseth him."

Happiness can only be found in a right relationship with our Lord. Paul said, "For the kingdom of God is not meat and drink; but righteousness, and peace, and joy in the Holy Ghost" (Romans 14:17). If a man is not at peace with God, at peace with himself, and at peace with his fellowman, and is not happy about it, if a person whose life is void of joy, then, he is not in the kingdom of God, even though he may be on his way to the kingdom of Heaven.

In John 3:3, Jesus said to Nicodemus, ". . . except a man be born again, he cannot see the kingdom of God." Many have preached that Nicodemus was a lost man. I don't believe so; let me tell you why.

When Jesus was speaking in John 6:44, He said, "no man can come to me except the Father which hath sent me draws him (by His Spirit)." When Jesus was talking to Peter, He said, ". . . Whom say ye that I am" (Matthew 16:15). Then Peter answered in verse 16, "Thou art the Christ, the Son of the living God." In verse 17, Jesus said, "Flesh and blood hath not revealed it unto thee, but my Father which is in heaven."

When Nicodemus came to Jesus, he said, "I know that thou art a teacher come from God." Nicodemus could not have known that Jesus was a teacher from God unless the Father revealed it to him.

Jesus tells us that it is the Father's good pleasure to give unto us the kingdom and all that is therein. (Luke 12:31-32) It makes our Father happy to give us those things that bring joy into our lives, like good health, peace, happiness, forgiveness, understanding, and anything else we require to be happy.

Jesus went on in the third chapter of John to reveal to Nicodemus about the Word and the Spirit. Jesus also said that the kingdom of God suffereth violence and the violent take it by force. (Matthew 11:12) What did He mean?

I believe He meant that there would be many who would not want to follow Christ into His kingdom here on earth because of the price they would have to pay; but, some would, so they would have to plow through those who would want them to stop or slow down. I believe it means that you and I must force our way through all the idiosyncrasies of our brothers and sisters in the Lord who have sat down, those who don't want to do this, or don't want to do that, who criticize this and condemn that.

You've got to put your head down like a football player and force your way through and say, "Listen, if you don't want to go on, sit where you are, but I'm going on."

A man once said to me, "Bill, I believe, but I just don't believe like you do."

"That's okay," I told him. "Don't worry about it. If you go to heaven we are going to have a wonderful time. If you go to hell, I ain't going to miss you!"

I went to the doctor to take an insurance physical to cover a note at the bank. When the doctor put the stethoscope on my chest, he said, "You seem to be at peace."

I said, "I am!"

"You even act like you are awfully calm."

"How can you tell that with a stethoscope?"

He asked just what I attributed my peace and calmness to, and I told him, "Christ Jesus."

"I don't believe that junk!" he retorted.

I said, "Doctor, what do I care whether you believe it or not? I'm the one who is at peace!"

I have never seen the Lord. I hear others talk about how Christ has appeared in their presence. I never deny their experience because a person "knows what he knows that he knows"; he knows it! I have never seen the Lord except in the Bible and in people. But do you want to know something else? I have never seen the devil either, except in people. And it doesn't take long to know who you are talking to!

I refuse to let somebody else's life bring me under bondage to their conscience.

The Lord is my shepherd, not the people.

The Lord is my provider.

The Lord is my comforter.

The Lord is my peace.

The Lord is my strength.

When you and I can feel an acceptance of one another as persons, regardless of our conflict over beliefs, we are going to love one another right where we are. We are not going to expect anybody to live the Christian life according to our expectations. We are going to love them right where they are. We are going to let them see Christ in us and hope that that they will accept the Christ that we serve so that we will all be together in the kingdom of heaven.

Furthermore, what can separate us from the love of God that is in Christ Jesus? Can principalities? Or powers?

Or life? Or death? A nagging wife? A cantankerous husband? An unruly son or daughter? The Lord says through his servant, Paul, that nothing is able to separate us from the love of God which is in Christ Jesus. (Romans 8:38) The only one who can separate me is ME, or separate you is YOU.

So my friend, if you and I don't feel close to the Lord and a part of His kingdom, then I ask you, "WHO MOVED?"

My Bible tells me how much God loves me. Wherever I look and wherever I open it, He tells me that He loves me. He gives me the opportunity to share this love with you. We can all be a part of the kingdom of God, because we are all children of God. AMEN!

8

God's Love Letter

If ye keep my commandments, ye shall abide in my love; even as I have kept my Father's commandments, and abide in his love. — John 15:10

Because of stubborn pride, nearly two miserable years of going from bad to worse had passed from the time the Lord first revealed Himself to me and when I accepted Him as Saviour and Lord. The Lord had revealed to me by His Spirit that I was lost, and that if I would open my heart to Him I would find the joy and the peace I sought. But, I was convinced that my wife had set me up for it and would not go forward when the minister gave the altar call.

Also, I had not learned at that point that it is the responsibility of God to reveal Himself to us and let us know who He is. Once He does that, it is our decision to accept or to reject Him.

The night I finally got up and went to the altar to make an outward confession of an inward work, the pastor came to me after the service and made a point of speaking to me privately for a moment. "Bill," he said to me, "do you have a Bible?"

"No," I replied, "I don't have a Bible; I don't know how to read a Bible. I don't understand the Bible; and in conclusion, I don't want a Bible."

I was very definite about the whole matter, but the Pastor was not the least bit impressed because he was under a conviction far stronger than mine.

"Oh yes, you have to have a Bible!" he told me. "I'm going to tell you — teach you how to read it."

That is exactly what he did by saying something to me that has stuck in my mind since that night and has had great meaning to me.

He said, "Know this, that God has cursed your flesh, 'from dust thou art, and to dust thou shalt return' (Genesis 3:19). This Bible, Bill, is not written to your flesh; it is written to your spirit. God sent the Holy Spirit to reveal the Christ of the Bible unto us." He then placed a King James version of the Holy Bible in my hands and closed his hands around mine. Looking directly at me with love shining from his heart, he continued, "I want you to take this Bible and I want you to read it as a love letter from God to you."

My mother-in-law once said to me, "Bill, do you mind if I give you some advice?"

I said back to her, "No, if you don't mind if I don't take it!" So, I give the same kind of advice to you. You don't have to take it. I won't get mad if you do or if you don't! The best advice I can give to you today is when you read the Bible, read it as a *love letter from God to you.* He loves you. Whether anybody else likes you or not is unimportant. God loves you! He says beware when all men speak well of you. "Woe unto you, when all men shall speak well of you! For so did their fathers to the false prophets" (Matthew 6:26). If everybody likes you, you are in trouble.

I want you to know that I was in the middle of the road until I discovered that there is that bunch of people over there who don't like me and this bunch over here likes me. Since I am casting the final ballot, I like *me,* too! I have decided to get with the group who does like me and I don't intend to waste my time with that other bunch!

Read your Bible as *a love letter from God* to you. Try to find out how much He loves you.

Now one other thing, when God talks about judgment, Reader, I pass right over that! Why? Because He isn't talking to me. I am His son, and He doesn't want me to be afraid of Him. He wants me to love Him, so, I take *His love letter,* in which He tells me that I am one of His children and He loves me, and I read it without fear or hesitation. "For ye are all the children of God by faith in Christ Jesus" (Galatians 3:26).

When I was in the "booze joints," I was minding my own business, bothering no one (or so I thought), but God stuck

His nose in my business. He told me I wasn't happy in my condition. He said, "You are not happy being a drunk."

Well, I really wasn't too happy when I was drunk, though I did feel happy because I was enjoying the pleasures of sin for a season. You can be happy drunk. When you are drunk you don't have a care in the world. You don't worry about things like "What did I do to make the boss so mad?", or your creditors, or your crying children, or your nagging wife.

Speaking of creditors, I would like to share this little story with you. At one time I owed my banker $3,000 and I couldn't pay him. I couldn't sleep at night because I owed him. So, I knocked on his door and said to him, "Hey, I owe you $3,000!"

"That's right," he answered.

"I can't pay you. But there isn't any sense of both of us worrying about it. You go ahead and do the worrying!"

I have owed bankers so much that when they asked, "How are you?", there was a look in their eyes that told me they really meant it! When my banker comes to a meeting where I am speaking, he isn't there to enjoy the meeting. He is there to check on my health! Actually my banker is not only a good banker, he is a good friend as well. We have had some great times of fellowship together.

You can be happy when you are drunk and you can be temporarily released from your worries, but the happiness you find in drink is short-lived. Christ provides a more lasting peace (and without the hangover!).

God loves you. He wants you to know Him. The Scriptures are written to you and me as individuals. There are many doctrines going around the world today, but I am so grateful for the knowledge that the Holy Spirit was not sent to protect me, but He was sent to reveal Christ Jesus unto me.

As the Holy Spirit reveals Christ unto us we begin to see Jesus as He is. Christ Himself said, these things that I do, Greater things shall you do. (John 14:12) Peter told us in Acts 2:39, concerning the Holy Ghost, ". . . the promise is unto you, and to your children, and to all that are afar off, even as many as the Lord our God shall call."

All He is waiting for is for you and me to exercise our faith and pray. He is the one who will meet our needs. There are many people with many needs. There are those who are unsaved that the Lord will save. There are those who are sick that the Lord will heal. There are those who are seeking to be filled with the Holy Spirit and the Lord will baptize them. Every need of every heart can and will be met if those seeking will exercise enough faith to receive what God wants to do for each individual.

There is not a man or woman who can do anything for you except pray for you. But when someone prays for you, he or she is obligating the Lord to honor His word. He said, "And these signs shall follow them that believe; In my name shall they cast out devils; they shall speak with new tongues" (Mark 16:17).

When I was on an evangelistic tour in Hawaii, a man came up to me and said, "Brother, the Lord told me that you are supposed to be under submission to me. You are to come and labor here in Hawaii."

"Brother," I replied, "in all due respect, I was talking to the Lord twenty minutes ago and He didn't even tell me that He knew you!"

Everyone seems to have the will of the Lord for somebody else, and they can't seem to find the will of the Lord for themselves. The Words of Jesus tell us, ". . . If ye continue in my word, then are ye my disciples indeed; And ye shall know the truth, and the truth shall make you free" (John 8:31-32). Then, we read in verse 36, "If the Son therefore shall make you free, ye shall be free indeed." We are not under bondage to men!

If I discern that your spirit is not open to the gospel of Jesus Christ, I am not under the bondage to believe that I have to cram the gospel down your throat. I only talk to people who are open to the gospel, when the Lord reveals to me that they are open to it. If the Lord reveals to me that you are not open to receive the gospel, I will talk to you about golf. I'll talk to you about fishing. I'll talk to you about anything you wish to talk about, but I ain't going to talk to you about Jesus.

When God gives me the knowledge about me, and when I see myself as I really am, I'll be the "biggest hypocrite going" if I condemn you for anything! The Apostle John writes, "My little children, these things write I unto you, that ye sin not. And if any man sin, we have an advocate with the Father, Jesus Christ the righteous: And he is the propitiation for our sins: and not for ours only, but also for the sins of the whole world" (I John 2:1-2).

People will try to bring you under bondage. They can't live the life themselves, but they will tell you how to live it. What you must do is just smile at them — with or without your teeth! I'm a Pollock full of Pollock jokes and without teeth of my own; so, I can get by with saying that!

When anybody gets upset over what you believe, it's because he or she doesn't know what he believes himself. When you know who you are, and you know where you are, and you know what you are doing, you know where you are going, it shouldn't bother you what anybody else believes.

Let me ask you, who really cares whether you live or die? Who really cares? Think about your friends; think about the people all around you. Who really cares whether you live or die?

How long do you think you are going to be remembered?

They are going to say, "Oh, wasn't she a nice lady," or "Wasn't he a nice man?", and six weeks later they forget you until someone comes along and says, "Hey, what ever happened to so and so?"

They will answer back, "Oh yeah, that's right, he passed away a couple of months ago."

Reader, do you know who really cares? Jesus cares. The Father loves you, and you must love yourself. If you don't think anything of yourself, nobody is going to. Don't be always wanting to put yourself down, because there are enough people willing to do that for you. Jesus said, ". . . thou shalt love the Lord thy God with all thy heart, and with all thy soul, and with all thy mind" (Matthew 22:37). And He tells us in verse 39, ". . . thou shalt love thy neighbor as thyself."

If you want to know what you think of yourself, ask your neighbor how you are treating him, because, Reader, when you see somebody with your faults, you can't stand them! That's why I say, "I must examine my own heart. I must take heed to my own ways. I must get along with myself." Examine your heart this very minute. Find out who you are at odds with, and ask yourself, "Who's at fault, them or me?"

God, by His Spirit, is going to speak to your heart (spirit). He is going to let you know how much He loves you, and how much He wants to do for you. He is no respector of persons. What He has done for one, He'll do for another.

The Lord is changing my life and ministry every day, and I have come to realize that my greatest responsibility of friendship is with me. I must get along with me. In order to get along with me, I have got to know me. I've got to continually look within to see who I really am. If I am at peace with God and at peace with myself, I will automatically be at peace with everyone else.

Consequently, I will never point my finger at you for anything you do, for anything you say, for any place you go. I will love you right where you are. I will love you whether you like me or not. No matter what you do, it will have no bearing on my love for you.

I learned a tremendous truth — my Father loves me. If He loved me many years ago when I first began to serve Him, how much more does He love me today?

So, my friend, God wants to reveal Himself unto you and to reveal you unto yourself. In love, He has for you the greatest love letter you will ever receive. As I did with the first Bible I ever owned, you take the Bible and read it as a LOVE LETTER TO YOU FROM GOD!

> *God is so good,*
> *God is so good,*
> *God is so good to me!*

LOVED BY THE FATHER*

There are times I feel that I'm so alone
    and that no one really cares.

There are times I think my heart will break,
    and I'm blinded by my tears.

There are times I feel that I'm so tired,
    and I must stop to rest,

But a still small voice within me cries,
    "our loving Father, He knows what's best."

Then a strength flows through my heart,
    as I praise the one I love,

As my Father said, "Take one more step
    toward your mansion up above.

Don't look at your heartaches and sorrows,
    don't dwell on the trials of life.

Be happy, be cheerful, put a smile on your face.
    You have been chosen to become the Lord's wife."

Oh, to be loved by the Father,
    because of our love for His Son.

Just to be lead by His Spirit,
    walking, with all three in one.

Now I shall never be lonely;
    I just have to remember this day,

That wherever I go and whatever I do,
    my Saviour has traveled this way.

9

Our Father's Love For Us

For God so loved the world, that he gave his only begotten Son, that whosoever believeth in him should not perish, but have everlasting life. John 3:16

When I let God take over my life and reveal Himself unto me, I found new ways of expressing myself. I found that I could be a general in God's army to win souls for Him. I found the joy of using humor to the glory of God. I found that the Holy Spirit can flow through me and help me express my thoughts and feelings in singing, speaking, and writing poetry — echoing in song, word and verse the love He has for me.

> *"Now Jesus is my Lord and my bridegroom.
> And oh, the love my Saviour gives to me;
> A love that wipes away all of my heartache,
> A love that has set my spirit free.
> His love is far greater than my expectations;
> His kindness, far beyond my fondest dreams.
> He walks with me and there's no condemnation,
> For I'm His bride, and I know that He loves me."

My smile became the fragrance of the Rose, the Rose of Sharon, Christ Jesus, who lives in my heart. I am happy today, but I am not happy because I am free from trouble. I am not happy because I have no trials or tribulations. I am happy because my Father loves me. It is the happiness that comes from knowing that you are loved. No matter where I go or what I do, He will never leave me nor will He forsake me, because He said, "And, lo, I am with you alway, even unto the end of the world" (Matthew 28:20).

While I was coming home from a two week evangelistic tour of Washington and Oregon, I stopped overnight to rest. Weary from speaking engagements and travel, I sat down on the floor of my lonely motel room between two beds, bracing my back on one, and propping my feet up on the other. I had just come from a restaurant where I had eaten a solitary meal.

"Lord," I said, "why can't I be a normal Christian, like other people?"

"What is a normal Christian?" the Word came back to me.

"One who has a job from eight to five o'clock, goes to church on Wednesday, teaches a Sunday School class on Sunday, and is able to stay home the rest of the days during the week."

As I sat here engulfed in waves of self-pity, having what I came later to call a "pity-party in the pity-pit," I suddenly was so overwhelmed with frustration that I took a paper and pencil from my briefcase and began to write. When the pencil stopped moving, I was amazed at what came "out of the pencil." On the paper were these words:

*YOU WILL NEVER BE

Do not think and time will have no meaning,
    Do not walk and time will be no more.
Do not wonder about small things or tomorrow,
    And you'll never know what life has in store.
Do not love and you shall know no heartache,
    Do not expect and disappointed you'll not be,
Do not give, you'll end up losing nothing.
    But you haven't lived, "So you will never be."

From that time on, every poem that I have had the privilege of writing has come out of an experience that the Lord and I have either been in ourselves, or we have counselled and talked with someone who has been there, or we have just gotten out of it — or we are getting ready to go into such an experience.

The assurance that the Father loves me gives me a peace that no one has ever been able to take from me. He introduced Himself to me by His Spirit. He gave me joy.

And in God there is no variance; what He has done for one, He will do for another. We are all children of God. "And if children, then heirs of God, and joint heirs with Christ . . ." (Romans 8:17).

The people who are unhappy today are those who want to be unhappy. The people who are down in the mouth are those who desire to feel sorry for themselves, to wallow in their own self-pity and have everybody catering to them, to get attention. We are what we want to be, but Christ wants us to be a joy for Him.

A lot of people go around looking like they have been baptized in lemon juice! If you've got to complain, if you've got to gripe about your relationship with Christ, don't tell anybody that you are a Christian, and they won't know the difference!

Know this, you can't blame your husband for your condition right now; you can't blame your wife for your condition right now; you can't blame your mother or your dad, your son or your daughter for your condition. You are an individual whom God has called personally, and how you live is your responsibility to God.

No person should be able to rob us of our joy in the Lord. Paul wrote in the book of Romans that nothing can separate us from the love of God that is in Christ Jesus. "For I am persuaded, that neither death, nor life, nor angels, nor principalities, nor powers, nor things present, nor things to come, Nor height, nor depth, nor any other creature, shall be able to separate us from the love of God, which is Christ Jesus our Lord" (Romans 8:38-39).

The only one who can separate me (you) from the love of God is me (you). That's why we can be happy in every situation of life, no matter how dark and dreary it is. We are in the hands of our Father. Our Father did not bring us this far to let us fail. He wants to reveal Himself to us, to let us know that He is our Father, that He loves us and that we can trust Him.

Christ is a personal Saviour and if we do not know Him personally, we do not know Him. It is not our place to reveal ourselves to God because He knows all there is to know about us, but it is the responsibility of God to reveal Himself to us. Once He does this, then we must make this decision, "Do we want to accept or do we want to reject Him?"

You see, if somebody wants you to follow him, I believe it is his responsibility to reveal himself to you before you follow him. If you walked into a bank and said to the president of that bank, "Please loan me some money because I am in great need of money," would the bank loan it to you on that basis?

NO! First, you would have to prove to the bank your ability to repay it. You would be "checked out" to find out who you are, what your credit rating is, and if you have the ability to repay the loan. Next, the bank officials would enter into a contract with you, and then you do business.

If the Lord wants us to do business with Him, I feel it is our responsibility to check Him out, to make sure we know who He is, who He represents Himself to be, and exactly who it is that we are following. God does not want us to follow Him blindly. God loves us that much that He will reveal Himself to us. He will prove Himself to you if you will let Him.

And how can we serve God in turn? What does He want from you and from me for all we receive from Him?

I'll never forget the time when I was troubled in my spirit. I listened to a man who preached on the text, "I would that you were cold or hot but because you are lukewarm, I am going to spew you out of my mouth." (Revelation 3:15-16) He preached the message in the way that so many people interpret those Scriptures. But, Reader, that text can't mean what people have tried to lead us to believe. Instead of helping me in my search for direction in my life, that preacher preached me under bondage with his sermon.

"Lord, how can I be hot?" I asked.

Who is hot today? Who do you know that's hot for God? I don't know today, or back through my years in Christ Jesus, of a man who is hot for God. If you took that Scripture the way that man was preaching it, it would be better to be cold and do nothing than it would be to strive to be hot and end up only lukewarm and get spewed out! The cold doesn't get spewed out; the hot doesn't get spewed; only the luke-warm get spewed out!

It can't mean what people try to lead us to believe: "Brother, I wish you were like I am; I wish you were doing what I am doing." NO! Listen, God loves you whether you do anything or not.

There is only one way that you and I can serve God — with our praise and gratitude for what He has done for us. It is the height of audacity to think that we can go out and serve somebody who has everything. God has the whole universe! And I am going out there and say, "Lord, you sure are lucky you called this 'Pollock.' Where would you be today if it weren't for me?"

Listen, the only way I can serve the Lord is with my heartfelt joy and praise for what He did even for me.

We have six children, several grandchildren. I remember when our oldest daughter got married. The usher brought the groom's mother down the aisle on his arm. Then, he escorted my wife to her proper place on the left side of the sanctuary. The wedding march began and I brought one of the pride and joy offspring from our nest down to stand in front of the minister.

"Who giveth this girl?" he asked with all the dignity of the Divine.

"Giveth nothing." I replied, "It cost me a thousand bucks!"

Whoever heard of giving them away? And do you know what she did when he pronounced the couple man and wife? She kissed me and her mother on the cheek and said, "Dad, bcause you have served me so faithfully, for the last twenty years, my husband and I are going to serve you for the next twenty years. You can expect a check the first of every month." Is that the way they do it?

NO! My daughter just said simply to me, "Thanks Dad, we love you very much," as she kissed me on the cheek.

I said, "WHAT! After twenty years of service all we receive is a "Thanks, Dad, we love you very much'?"

I'll never forget the first diaper I changed for her. I'd pick up her legs, wipe her backside with a washcloth, get ready to pull up the diaper after I sprinkled her with baby powder. I would get ready and what would she do? She would fill it up again! I had to ask my wife, "How do you turn it off?" Five times she did that to me! And you could never imagine how something so sweet could stink so bad! I used to turn my head and suck in the deepest breath my lungs could hold, and hold that breath until my lungs nearly exploded until I'd get it all done!

But, you know, after we'd get the diaper pinned up, we would forget that she had dirtied it in the first place.

That is the way we should do with the mistakes of one another. We are just children of God. When we make a mistake, the powder of the Holy Spirit can make us sweet in the Lord. Let us forget we made a mistake in the first place and just go right on from there.

With all the time that we served her, after 20 years of loyal service, all we received was a, *"Thanks, Dad, I love you very much."* And you know — *that was enough.* That was all I wanted her to do or say.

What does the Father want to hear from us?

When He does something for us, He wants to hear us say, "Thanks, Dad, we love you very much." Reader, the *doing* just *comes automatically.* The *doing will come with joy;* the *service* comes in *gratitude* and *being thankful for what He has done for us.*

If someone came up to one of my children and asked, "Why are you so happy?", I would love to hear him or her say, "My Daddy loves me." I don't want my children to fear me, to cower down every time I walk into their presence. Instead, I want my children to love me and the only way they can love me is by my first loving them.

That is the only way my children can really serve me, and do you know? The only service that you and I can render to God is when we tell people of His love.

Sometimes no one asks us why we are happy, because we never seem to be happy. Whenever someone comes up and asks, "How are you?", *if we tell them they soon quit asking!* But, when someone does ask us why we are happy when we are happy, and when our *"happy"* is *so happy* that *if their "happy" isn't as happy as our "happy"* that they feel miserable, then, we should tell them, "My Daddy loves me." Our heavenly Father wants us to know and feel His love, and love Him and others in turn. I feel that He does not want us to fear Him.

I have found that in my own life it isn't *what I do* that is important. It is *what I am* that's important.

At this writing I am an international director for the Full Gospel Businessmen's Fellowship International. Every man who serves in the FGBMFI is serving in the position he is presently serving because he said that he would like to serve in that position. If at any time any of these men don't like what they are doing (whether it is ushering, greeting, sitting at the table) all he has to do is say, "I don't want to do it," and he doesn't have to do it again. We accept his resignation immediately. A guy has only to mention one time, "I don't like what I'm doing," and he won't be doing it anymore! But, if he is doing what he thinks he is qualified to do, and he doesn't do it the way the other men think he should be doing it, we get rid of him anyway! After all, there is no sense in him making us miserable!

The above is just a funny side comment: *the point is, every man does what he wants to do and enjoys doing it.* All the FGBMFI men are happy in serving the Lord. I believe that is what God wants you and me to do because He is equally happy doing things for us.

A few years ago, I had an old 1967 Ford that needed new tires, a new battery, plugs, points, a condenser, and new brakes. I took that old car down to Pensiton and McGee Alignment Service, on Central Street in Wichita, Kansas. I asked the mechanic if he would fix my car for me. I was going to give it to my daughter. He said he would and told me approximately how much it would cost to fix it.

"How much do I owe you?" I asked when I went back to pick up the car.

"Tell you what," he replied, looking at me directly (with tongue in cheek), "Why don't you go ahead and take the car. If I send you a bill, I'll send it to the FGBMFI and you can send me a receipt. You don't have to worry about paying for it!"

Now I was grateful for that! (that's why I just gave him a commercial!) He is a fine Christian man. I drove the car home, excited about being able to give it to my daughter. It wasn't much, but it was what I could afford to give her, and I was so happy to know that I had something to offer her.

What do you think she said? Did she come back with a snippy retort like, "Do you honestly think I am going to drive around in that old piece of junk? Do you think I want an old broken down heap like that? Daddy! Why can't I have a new one?"

NO! She loved that old car and affectionately named it her "Big Tank." It doesn't have power steering, and she says that she gets her exercise driving it!

I have known more joy out of doing that for her than anything. If, however, she refused to accept it, I would have been hurt. Another daughter of mine meets me at the door and confiscates all of my pennies, which she puts in a big jar. It brings me joy to do things for my children. How much more does it make our heavenly Father happy to do things for us? He wants us to be happy. When we don't let God give unto us, we rob Him of a blessing. The hardest thing for you and I to do is to learn to receive.

"ONE DAY AT A TIME"

One day at a time is all I must walk,
　　Then my vision will never be blurred,

For the Lord promised me that I'll always see
　　if I walk, just one day, in His Word.

Tho' friends pass me by and someday I might cry,
　　And wonder why I have a troubled mind,

Jesus whispered, "Look above, let me fill your heart
　　with love.
　　Walk with Me, just one day at a time."

So down life's path I go, as I walk both to and fro,
　　To everyone I meet I shall be kind,

As Christ's Spirit flows within a hungry heart that's free
　　from sin.

　　I'll walk with Jesus, just one day at a time."

10

Freed From Bondage

If the Son therefore shall make you free, ye shall be free indeed. John 8:36

I would like to live my life in such a way that even the undertaker will be sorry when I pass away! I talk many times about life and death. I am known as the "death speaker," and the reason is that I believe if Jesus tarries, we are all going to die.

If I thought that I would have to spend 150 to 200 years on this earth, I don't think I could stand it . . . *Rigor mortis* has already set in and I am glad!

My hair is falling out; my teeth have already fallen out — uppers and lowers! In fact, when I got up this morning, I looked in the mirror and said, "Well, good morning, Tiger!"

"Put my teeth in, will you?" the image growled at me.

"You will get your teeth when I am ready to put them in, and not before!" I retorted.

"Please, can't you put my teeth in?" whined the poor creature with his nose sitting on his chin!

Have you ever seen a *Pollock* with no teeth? If you haven't, I tell you — you "ain't lived!" You haven't lived until you look into a mirror without your teeth. If you have false teeth, you know what I'm talking about, right?

When you go some place and you see all those bald-headed men (perhaps like me, you are one of them!), it looks like heaven, "there will be no parting there!" You see those little girls all dolled up in ribbons and lace, or skinny little things in blue jeans, and you know they haven't got a chance. They are going to turn into fat, old women! You don't believe me? Look around you, how many fat, old women can you think of? You see, our bodies are dying and there is not a thing we can do about it.

When my wife and I are fighting, we don't even soak our teeth in the same glass!

Speaking of fighting . . . a little sidelight to let you know we talk the same language, and to give you something to relate to, when we are getting along, we sleep in a kingsize bed. It is like sleeping in a meadow. When we go to sleep at night, I hook my left ankle around hers and we go to sleep. Some people suck their thumbs! Some have a security blanket! But me, I hook my ankle around her! But, when we are fighting, I get over on the far side of the bed, and she gets clear over on the other side, and I don't get one minute's sleep because I am afraid that if I go to sleep, I'll roll over and automatically hook my ankle around hers, and she will think I'm making up!

But anyway, Reader, we are dying and there is not a thing we can do about it. You may not die of cancer; you may not die in a plane crash; you may not die of tuberculosis, but if Jesus tarries you are going to die of old age, and there isn't a thing you can do about it.

The body tries to place great demands upon us: he is dying. It thrills me to know he is dying; so, I am not going to waste too much time on him. What makes me feel so good when I look over a congregation where I am speaking and see all the grey-headed, fat people (when I mention this it brings some laughter and a few chuckles but the fat people are usually the ones who aren't laughing!) is to realize the mercy of our Lord. If Jesus tarries, they are going to lay your body in the ground and you are going to be gone.

He says I may let you live to the age of 70. If that happens (at this writing), I have 25 years to go. I may make it and I may not. If Christ tarries, I know that I am going to die, and I'm looking forward to it with such joy that I make fun of my body every day. You know, he always likes to think he is strong and handsome and good looking. I stand sideways in front of the mirror and he's got nothing but a big pouch, that broad chest that he is bragging about has dropped three feet on him! So, I tell you, I don't spend too much time with somebody who doesn't look too hot! I don't give him too much of my time. I do not have to let him put me into bondage.

My body is important in this life because it is the temple of the Holy Ghost, and we are to glorify God in our body, but "What? know ye not that your body is the temple of the Holy Ghost which is in you, which ye have of God, and ye are not your own? For ye are bought with a price: therefore glorify God in your body, and in your spirit, which are God's" (I Corinthians 6:19-20). We are not to worship our body and let it become dominant over our lives. "For to be carnally minded is death; but to be spiritually minded is life and peace" (Romans 8:5).

Another thing, I will not condemn myself for anything that I allowed to happen in my life; furthermore, I am not going to let anyone else condemn me for it either.

Today is all you have. Yesterday is past and there is not a thing you nor I can do about it. It is over and done. So, I forgive myself for everything I did yesterday, because ". . . happy is he that condemneth not himself in that thing which he alloweth" (Romans 14:22).

In the years that I have been preaching, there has not been one drunk come up to me and say, "Ge-rosky, I—don't like what youu're pre-ching!" (I can talk like that because I used to be one of them.) You know who don't like what I am talking about? The Christians who have been trying to bring me under bondage, the people who are not at peace with themselves. They are not at peace with their fellowman. They are always griping and complaining about something. You show me somebody who is always griping about something and I will show you somebody who doesn't have it all together for himself.

People will always try to bring you under subjection to their conscience. They will always try to tell you what God's will is for you, and they can't seem to find it for themselves.

ANYTHING THAT BRINGS YOU UNDER BONDAGE IS NOT OF GOD, whether it is a man or a woman, a job, a community, a Full Gospel organization, or the misunderstanding of the meaning of the Scriptures. God did not call us to be under bondage. He called us to be free. Where the kingdom is, there is liberty and freedom — freedom from sickness, freedom from strife, freedom from heartache, and freedom from sorrow. ". . . Not by might, nor by power, but by my spirit, saith the Lord of hosts" (Zechariah 4:6).

Since I have become a Christian, since the Lord delivered me out of Egypt, out of my sins, the "Christians have been trying to take me back to Egypt." Not the drunks, not the gamblers, not the derelicts, but my Christian friends have been trying to place me back under bondage. They try to bring me under subjection under their conscience and they have a form of external holiness that because I would not adhere to what they were trying to tell me to do, they ostracized themselves from me. Is that what a holy person would do? No, that's what a hypocrite trying to be holy would do. They try to take me back into bondage and want me to live my life according to their standards. I can't live according to their standards. I can't live according to your standards. And I want you to know I don't intend to; I am going to go right on making some beautiful mistakes.

Each night in my bedroom, or motel room, I take all the mistakes that I made that day, and I stuff them down at the foot of the bed, underneath. You know, I'd sure like to see someone's face when she wheels back those sheets and sees all my mistakes lying there at the bottom!

Each morning when I get up, I take a big deep breath (cough a little!) of fresh air, and begin looking forward to all the mistakes I will make today. I have made about 26 already, and I have learned so much from making those mistakes. I have learned because I know that all I have to do is live only with *these mistakes now*. Tonight I am going to bury them, because I cannot carry the mistakes of yesterday, the mistakes I am going to make today, and the mistakes I think I am going to make tomorrow. I can't bring them all into *now* and make it through the day. I've got to shed something; so, I shed yesterday, I shed tomorrow, and I am just a *happy Pollock* today!

Paul says, "And because of false brethren unawares brought in, who came in privily to spy out our liberty which we have in Christ Jesus, that they might bring us into bondage: To whom we gave place by subjection, no, not for an hour; that the truth of the gospel might continue with you" (Galatians 2:4-5). In other words, "I will not come under subjection to another man's conscience." People are talking today about *what was*. They feel that we should witness to what has already happened in our lives. Reader, what the Lord is looking for today is people who are talking about *what is*.

When people stand to testify, they say, "Twenty-five years ago. . . ." The Lord isn't interested in what went on twenty-five years ago. He says if Christ be in us we will be a new creature. Yesterday will pass away and behold today we will become new in Christ. (II Corinthians 5:17). Yesterday is gone. The question is: What are we today in Christ Jesus? I realize that if I were God (which you should be glad I am not, because He has been blessing some of you people I wouldn't think of blessing!) I would reveal myself to you and keep on leading you as a child is led by his father.

If God wants us to know something about Him, He must reveal Himself to us. But, I want you to know I am not going to sit around *piddling* my fingers saying, "Oh God, are you going to show me something today?" Instead I am going to live today to the best of my ability and if He wants me to know something He is going to have to show me. I am not going to worry about where I am, where I am not, where I have been, or where someone thinks I should be. I just know who I am; I know where I am; I know what I am doing; and I know where I am going.

The Lord may not be interested in what happened 25 years ago in my life, only what is going on today, but sometimes He will use the knowledge of how He revealed Himself to someone in the past as a teaching for someone.

People insist, "You've got to serve the Lord! You must serve the Lord!" You know what? How can you serve the Lord according to somebody else's dictation?

I am grateful that in the kingdom of God, we can have peace and joy in the Holy Ghost. I am grateful that we can be joyful, happy, in our walk with the Lord. Sometimes we are so busy doing that we have forgotten how to be joyful.

Acts 1:8 says, "But ye shall receive power, after that the the Holy Ghost is come upon you: and ye shall be witnesses unto me both in Jerusalem, and in all Judaea, and in Samaria, and unto the uttermost part of the earth." If we will be a

witness unto Christ today, then all of our tomorrows are
going to be happy ones; we will (in our happiness) automatically be a witness unto those with whom we come in
contact. We will not have to put other people under any
kind of bondage.

I have quit *trying to do*. I want to *try to be* what Christ
would have me to be. Jesus said, "Nevertheless I tell you
the truth; It is expedient for you that I go away: for if I go
not away, the Comforter will not come unto you; but if I
depart, I will send him unto you" (John 16:7). He will not
only be with you, but He shall be in you a well of living
water, springing up into life everlasting. He also said, "How-
beit when he, the Spirit of truth, is come, he will guide you
into all truth: for he shall not speak of himself; but whatsoever he shall hear, that shall he speak: and he will shew
you things to come. He shall glorify me: for he shall receive
of mine, and shall shew it unto you" (John 16:13-14).

My friend, Jesus has freed us. Freed us from our sin.
Freed us from our bodies that try to control us. Freed us
from the bondage of others, and He gave us forgiveness for
our mistakes. He gave us the Spirit of truth to dwell in us
as a well of living water, to show us that which God has
prepared for us who love Him for the Spirit searcheth all
things, yea, the deep things of God.

"Stand fast, therefore, in the liberty wherewith Christ
hath made us free, and be not entangled again with the yoke
of bondage" (Galatians 5:1).

> "You cannot change what happened
> yesterday, and you don't know what
> is going to happen tomorrow; so,
> if you will live today well as unto
> Christ, all of your tomorrows will
> be happy ones."*

"Brethren, I count not myself to have apprehended: but
this one thing I do, forgetting those things which are behind, and reaching forth unto those things which are before,
I press toward the mark for the prize of the high calling of
God in Christ Jesus" (Philippians 3:13-14).

11

We Are His Bride

. . . Turn, O backsliding children, saith the Lord: for I am married unto you. Jeremiah 3:14

I spend a lot of time in cemeteries — that's a fact! The cemetery is a quiet place to meditate. All the people who are there don't disturb me. They don't get upset if I want to praise the Lord, if I want to sing, or if I want to meditate upon the things of the Lord. I have no problems in the cemetery!

However, one day when I was out in a cemetery, I did run across a guy who was moaning and groaning. He was draped over a grave and in a shrill, grief stricken voice he kept repeating, "Why did you die? Oh, why did you die?"

I went up to him and, being the kind, considerate, lovable man that I am, I laid my hand on his shoulder and asked, "Is this your wife?"

"Oh, no!" he answered, "That's her first husband! . . . Oh, why did you die?"

I have met many people in all my years as a Christian, I have counseled with many husbands, many wives, many sons, many daughters, and many parents and their children. I know that not all marriages are made in heaven. I know that there are a lot of couples married today who are merely living together, just enduring one another, having no peace, no joy, and no happiness.

I also know that there is a doctrine going around today which instructs, "Wives, be subjective to your own husbands." One of the things I have been thinking about in the serenity of a quiet cemetery is a "wife's place," who a person really is, and what is a wife or a bride.

Reader, if you are a woman, do you know that you are a member of the body of Christ? Do you know that you have been loved by the Spirit of the Lord? Do you believe that the husband and wife are as one?

The Bible says that there is no marrying nor is there any giving in marriage in heaven. (Matthew 22:30)

I could never see how you could divide "one" without hurting both halves. So, I have puzzled over this statement in the Bible. What does it mean?

This is the result of my thinking. First, in counseling with husbands and wives, I have found that as a man I am also a bride of Christ. I am His wife, and He is my bridegroom. I must be subjective to my bridegroom, who is Christ. Second, I feel that the wife must also be subjected to the bridegroom, who is Christ. In short, we are all brides of Christ — men and women alike. In all marriages in which there are problems, you will find the source of the trouble if you will just search and find out which partner is not being subjective to Christ. When the wife is subjected to the bridegroom, and the husband is subjected to the bridegroom, then, the two are truly one in Christ Jesus. Everything else in their lives will then fall into place. But, when one or the other is not subjected to Christ, the two are not subjected to each other.

I, for one, would not want anyone to do anything for me unless it was out of a heart of love. I would not want anybody — a friend, a man, a woman, a relative, wife, husband, son or daughter — to do any thing for me that they did not want to do. When it is out of the heart of love, you can receive it or reject it, but the one who is giving it is the one who is blessed in the giving.

In my life, Jesus, who is my Bridegroom, gives with a perfect love and with no strings attached. He loves solely. He loves completely. He loves the spirit, soul, and the body. His love is not based upon what I am or what I do, but it is based upon His love for me and for you. God is no respector of persons; what He will do for one, He will do for others.

God will meet your needs and He will meet my needs, NOW, this very day. He is going to love us. He is going to bless us and administer unto us as individuals, whom He loves very much. He so loved you and I that He gave a bridegroom. If we would just let Him love us so that we can

love Him in return we will not perish but will have everlasting life and joy on this earth.

"Lord," I asked, "how, just how can I love you when
I really don't know how to love. How can I love my brothers
and sisters whom I have seen and let my heart say, 'I love
you' to you whom I have not seen?"

Our Lord said to me, "Do you know how you can love
me? The only way you can love me is through another person. The only way a person will know how much of my love
you have is by the way you treat him or her."

The only way I can give my love to God is by giving it
to you, to all those I come in contact with. I give my love
to Him by being kind to each person, by being considerate
and understanding, but most of all by forgiving.

You may not want my love; you may not want my
friendship. You may not want my kindness or whatever
I have to give you. But if you don't want it, I am not the
loser, you are. A person who does not want what you have
to give is the loser; you are not, because you know you are
willing to give it. They must be willing to receive it. If they
don't receive it, they have lost.

What have they lost? They have lost a part of you, that
part which you tried to give them.

How many times have you started out making a relationship with someone, had a friend in the making, but because
of a word that was spoken the wrong way, because of something that they did that you did not approve of, that you
did not like, you turned your back upon that person, severed
the relationship? Robbed yourself of what that person could
give in spite of his or her faults, in spite of their failures,
and in spite of the idiosyncrasies that you couldn't tolerate?

If we separate ourselves from another person because
of that, we are the loser. No matter who the person is, they
can give us something. They can do something for us. But if
a person is self-righteous, wrapped up in his own spiritual
importance, thinking that God can't get along without him,
that the program is going to fall unless he takes care of it,
he is a deceived person. He has robbed himself of the blessing of the multitude of God's people.

I know that this book has either been placed in your hands, or you have picked it up to read it, because of your searching for yourself or someone else. Perhaps you have a marriage that is on the "rocks" or you know of someone whose marriage is in trouble. If you are pondering in your hearts, "Which way will I turn? What will I do?" If you are the one with a husband or wife that you don't feel loves you, be of good cheer; there is no marrying or giving of marriage in Heaven. You have only to put up with him or her for only a few more years! The Lord is coming, and you have all eternity to spend without your spouse!

Even in that situation you can find peace and comfort. May I share a poem with you.

"FOR GOD SO LOVED*

For God so loved the man He created
    He placed him upon this lovely earth.

He wanted him to be His great champion;
    But this can only be, by the second birth.

He wanted him to know no pain or sorrow.
    He wanted him to know the joys of life.

He wanted him to know the thrill of loving,
    So God made for a man a loving wife.

So, if you and I, who may be man or woman,
    If we've learned the secret how to give our love;

We know the precious gift that we are giving
    was given to each of us from God above.

So, if you are a man with a woman who loves you.
    Who makes you happy on this road you trod,

Just lift your voice in praise and adoration,
    For she was sent to you from Christ, our God.

But, if you are a man or woman,
    Who has no place or love in which to hide,

Just lift your heart above the great horizon.
    For there is one who's calling you to be His bride.

Now Jesus is my Lord and my Bridegroom,
    And oh, the love my Saviour gives to me;

A love that wipes away all of my heartache,
    A love that set my spirit free.

His love is far greater than my expectations;
    His kindness, far beyond my fondest dreams,

He walks with me and there's no condemnation,
    For I'm His bride, and I know that He loves me."

Jesus says there is no condemnation to them who are in Christ Jesus for we have passed from death unto life. (John 5:24)

You and I are not condemned if we are in Christ Jesus. "For God sent not his Son into the world; but that the world through him might be saved" (John 3:17). Furthermore, if we are in Christ Jesus, neither should we condemn one another. There is no condemnation to them who are in Christ Jesus. Therefore, if condemnation flows forth from your lips or mine today, or at any other time, it might be because we "ain't where we think we are" with God!

We are instructed, "Brethren, if a man be overtaken in a fault, ye which are spiritual, restore such an one in the spirit of meekness; considering, thyself lest thou also be tempted" (Galations 6:1).

Don't push people down. Don't condemn them in their weakness. Instead, lift them up in your strength. Don't knock them down because they have failed, because they have not lived a life according to your expectations. Instead, pick them up in spite of their faults, in spite of their failures, saying to them by your actions, "I want you to know that God has brought me through it; I am a little stronger than I was the day before. Let me walk with you."

You say, "I just don't condone what that man is doing." Jesus didn't condone the activities of the publicans and sinners either, but He went anyway to eat with them. He went to minister to them as a physican ministering to the sick. He went because He loved them. He went because He knew who He was. He knew where He was. He knew what He was doing, and He knew where He was going. He knew that that person could not rob Him of that which God had given Him. He went to love His brother as He had been loved by the Father.

The only reason that you and I will pull ourselves away from another person's presence is because of what they are doing in their life. We are afraid we are not where we think we are, and we are going to fall. The only way we can make ourselves feel good is when we are saying something bad about someone else. We think, "If they don't look so good, maybe I won't look so bad. Maybe I'll seem a lot better than I am. If I can keep everybody looking at you, no one will have time to examine me and what I have been doing."

I have made a purpose in my life. When people start pointing their finger at somebody else in my presence, I start looking at the life of the person doing the pointing. I know the reason he or she is doing it: that person is trying to hide something.

Christ said, "This is my commandment, That ye love one another, as I have loved you" (John 15:12).

Have you ever prayed, "Lord, teach me how to love?" And you go out the next day and meet somebody who is unlovely. You cry, "Lord, I don't think you understood my prayer! Send me somebody who is going to teach me how to love!"

The Lord tells you, "I did. I sent you an unlovely person. How else are you going to know how capable you are of loving?"

Have you ever prayed for patience, and the next day you received tribulation? You cry out to the Lord, "But, Lord, I want patience!"

He replies, "But don't you know that tribulation worketh patience? And patience, hope?" (Romans 5:3)

Speaking of loving and having patience, if you let people get on your nerves, how foolish you are. Look at it this way. If I let you get on my nerves, it will give me a nervous stomach. A nervous stomach will turn to ulcers, the ulcers will turn to cancer, and cancer will kill me! I'll be out there in a graveyard buried and you will still be here to get on somebody else's nerves!

Reader, don't let anybody get on your nerves because it only destroys you when you do.

A woman came to my office one time and said, "I want to apologize to you."

"Why?" I asked.

"I have hated your guts for a year," she said.

I knew the woman and I knew where she'd been, but I queried, "Where have you been the past year?"

"Oh, it's been terrible," she replied, "I have been in the psychiatric ward for six months."

"You know," I said, "I have been to Florida twice, to California once; I went deep sea fishing in Corpus Christi, Texas, and also golfed there twice a week. You hated my guts! It drove you nuts! It didn't bother me a bit!"

Reader, if you don't like somebody, go tell them! There's no sense of you suffering alone! Haven't you ever wondered how you could dislike somebody so much and they seem so happy? It's because they think you are "kooky!" They don't know you don't like them.

"Love one another as I have loved you," the Lord gently commands us. Do you want someone to think that the Lord doesn't love you very much? If you and I can't deal with other people and our relationships with them in a loving way, we certainly aren't giving much evidence of the love the Father has given us. We need to ". . . forbear one another in love; endeavouring to keep the unity of the Spirit in the bond of peace" (Ephesians 4:3-4).

Only the other person is qualified to tell you or me how much love you or I have for our Lord because that person is the recipient of any of His love that we are showing. You see, when you know Christ, and you know yourself, when you are at peace with Christ and with yourself, nothing can upset you. Nothing can rob you of that peace. It is only when you don't know where you are that you have problems, especially when you see someone with your faults — you can't stand them!

Jesus is our bridegroom and we are His bride. He says He wants to give to us but He wants us to ". . . ask and ye shall receive, that your joy may be full" (John 16:24). He tells us that we have not because we ask not. (James 4:2)

Be sure of this — whatever you ask, that is just what you are
going to get, nothing more, nothing less. Everything we pray
for is what we receive. If we ask our Lord for one dollar and
we need five dollars, one dollar is all we will receive! If we
need healing and all we ask for is the strength to endure
the illness, the Lord may in His mercy heal you anyway,
but all you have coming is the strength to endure!

God tells us in *His love letter* to us to start asking and
don't worry about what other people think or what other
people say. If we give good gifts to our children, how much
more the Father wants to do for us. (Matthew 7:11) We are
asked to come and partake of the wedding feast but if we
will not come, we denounce and scoff at the invitation,
others will be asked in our place. (Matthew 22:8-9)

"And the Spirit and the bride say, Come. And let him
that heareth say, Come. And let him that is athirst come.
And whosoever will, let him take the water of life freely"
(Revelation 22:17). God is no respector of persons; His love
is for everyone. However, it is to be shared and passed on,
not kept to ourselves. "He that hath the bride is the bridegroom: but the friend of the bridegroom, which standeth
and heareth him, rejoiceth greatly because of the bridegroom's voice: this my joy therefore is fulfilled" (John 3:29).
We rejoice in the success of God's kingdom. He must increase
and we must decrease.

While I was in Corpus Christi, Texas, I not only went
deep sea fishing and played golf, I also spent time sitting on
the beach, thinking. Sitting by the ocean, I watched the
water as it moved over the sand, wave after wave. Birds
were walking on the sand leaving their footprints, but as
each wave came in, it washed away all traces of the birds'
footprints.

I thought of how the Spirit of the Lord comes into our
lives, to wash away all of our guilt, our heartaches and
sorrows. He wants us to be at peace with Him and at peace
with ourselves, and then we shall be at peace with our fellow
man. My friend, as you and I start each new day in prayer
to our Lord, accept His love, His forgiveness, and His
strength for this day.

"MAY WE ALL BE WITH GOD'*

Down by the ocean I sit today,
  Watching the waves roll in—

With a heart filled with love and praise to my Lord
  For there is no one with me, but Him.

The sound of the water rushing over the sand,
  How smooth is the path in its way.

It makes me so glad, this few moments I had,
  to be with my Saviour today,

My heart is so warm as I watch the waves roll.
  It seems they are trying to say,

"The heartaches and sorrow you feel in this life,
  It won't be long till they're all washed away."

So roll on and on, as you see the waves roll,
  The path you have chosen to trod.

Teaching His Word to those who've not heard,
  That in the end, we may all be with God."

12
Called To Witness

But the Lord said unto me, Say not, I am a child:
for thou shalt go to all that I shall send thee, and what-
soever I command thee thou shalt speak. Jeremiah 1:7

When I read the above scripture, I am reminded of when
I was first invited to speak before a group of people. Only
a short time before I became a Christian I had spent three
months in the psychiatric ward of Wesley Hospital in Wichita, Kansas, for attempted suicide. Needless to say, "I didn't
know nuthin' from nuthin'." Before that, I had served in
the Army and the Navy, and as I told you before, I have only
an eighth grade education.

But when I found Christ as my Saviour on October 3,
1954, the covenant that was true 2,000 years ago was just
as true for me at that moment. He poured out His Spirit
2,000 years ago and I was able to be filled with that same
Spirit in 1954.

I remember when I was asked to speak for the first time
in front of an audience. I said simply, "Lord, I am not a
speaker. I cannot speak. I don't know nothin' about nothin'.
I don't know your Word. I never read the Bible until I became a Christian. I didn't know anything about your Word.
I didn't know anything about the Spirit of God. I am not a
speaker . . . I can't go."

The preacher who had asked me to stand up and witness
of that which the Lord had recently done for me wouldn't
accept my answer. He insisted that I go home and pray
over the matter.

I went to a quiet place and dropped to my knees with
all my excuses reeling in my mind. However, a part of my
being wanted this opportunity to tell the world about the
Father who could love me (the unlovable).

When I had finished telling the Lord how inadequate I
was for the task, I entered into a covenant with the Lord.

"They say you are a God of miracles and can do many
things," I told the Lord. "That being so, if you will give me
the message I need tonight, I'll never ask for an opportunity

to speak. Every invitation I receive to speak I will take as coming from you. I will believe that you will not only give me the message I need for that moment, but you will also confirm your Word with signs following."

Rising to my feet, I knew that that night could have been my first and last opportunity to talk about Jesus. But when I stepped behind the pulpit at the Union Rescue Mission in Wichita, Kansas, it was a though as scroll in my mind's eye began to turn and I couldn't read it fast enough. It was as if I was standing back listening to what I was saying. For 45 minutes, I read that scroll. I knew when to quit. I turned and sat down.

"Give an altar call!" I heard a voice whisper in my ear.

"A what?" I asked, not comprehending.

"Give an altar call," C. W. Brown, the man who had gone with me, repeated.

"What do you mean?"

"Ask if anyone wants to get saved!" he said and almost lifted me bodily back onto my feet.

The room was so quiet my footsteps almost echoed off the walls as I walked back to the pulpit and said in an off-handed manner, "Anybody here wanta get saved?" Now, you know you can't make it any plainer than that! There is no working up to it, there is no beating around the bush. You either want to go to heaven or you are going to hell.

Some drunk got up in the very back row. He took three steps forward and two steps sideways. When he got to the front he looked up and said, "You me-ean-n to tell-me, that what-the-Lord-did-for-you . . . he'll do-o fer me?"

"That's right."

"What'll I havta do?"

I said, "Drop to your knees."

The man dropped to his knees, and C. W. Brown and I prayed for him for about 30 seconds. When that man stood up, HE STOOD UP STONE SOBER.

I walked away from that place knowing that from that moment on I would "study to show myself approved unto God, a workman that needeth not to be ashamed, rightly dividing the word of truth" (II Timothy 2:15).

I had made a covenant with the Lord. He had kept His part of the contract. He had showed me the way. He had revealed Himself unto me and let me know what He would have me to do.

Now it was my turn to uphold my part of the covenant. Every chance I got, I read. I studied, and I listened. I was taught by people; I was taught by preachers; I was taught by laymen; I was taught by women; I was taught by the Spirit of the Lord. Every person I talked to I would glean the good from their conversation. I would let the chaff fall by the wayside. I did not condemn a single person for that which I did not agree with. I only accepted that which I agreed with knowing that the Lord says, "As new born babes, desire the sincere milk of the Word, that ye may grow thereby" (I Peter 2:2).

As a new born babe in Christ, I was taught by the Holy Spirit. I John 2:27 told me: "But the anointing which ye have received of him abideth in you, and ye need not that any man teach you: but as the same anointing teacheth you of all things, and is truth, and is no lie, and even as it hath taught you, ye shall abide in him."

I loved the Lord and wanted to do everything I could for Him in return for all that He had done for me, knowing it would never be enough. But, I felt inadequate, unprepared for the course I was taking. Again, I got down on my knees and said, "Lord, Lord, I cannot speak! I am but a child! A new born babe in your kingdom."

But the Lord said unto me, "Say not that I am a child, for thou shall go to all that I shall send thee, whatsoever I command thee, thou shall speak." He said, ". . . be not afraid of them, neither be afraid of their words, though briers and thorns be with thee, and thou dost dwell among scorpions: be not afraid of their words, nor be dismayed at their looks, though they be a rebellious house" (Ezekiel 2:6). He was saying, "Be not afraid of their faces for I am with thee to deliver thee. Don't be afraid of whom you are talking to. Don't be afraid of where you are going, what you are going to say. I am going to deliver you out of their hands."

Then the Lord put forth His hand and He touched my mouth saying unto me, "Behold, I have put my Word in thy mouth."

Now, when you and I speak our opinion, it doesn't matter too much, BUT, when you and I speak, "Thus sayeth the Word of God," IT AMOUNTS TO EVERYTHING! The anointing may not be on Bill Gebrosky; the anointing may not be on you, but the anointing will always be on the Gospel of Jesus Christ! Paul said, "For I am not ashamed of the Gospel of Christ: for it is the power of God unto salvation to every one that believeth; to the Jew first, and also to the Greek" (Romans 1:16). And from the Apostle John: "But as many as received him, to them gave he power to become the sons of God, even to them that believe on his name" (John 1:12).

"See, I have this day set thee over the nations and over the kingdoms, to root out, and to pull down, and to destroy, and to throw down, to build and to plant" (Jeremiah 1:10). The Lord said all these things to the prophet, Jeremiah, when he received his call to the Lord's service, as recorded in the above scripture. He said them again to me as I, too, answered and hearkened to the Lord's ways.

God tells us throughout His Holy Word — His love letter to us — the importance of witnessing of Him who dwells within. He also tells us that our witness must be tempered with His Love.

How do we know that we are His disciples?

"By this shall all men know that ye are my disciples, if ye have love one to another" (John 13:35).

Where does this love come from?

"Beloved, let us love one another: for love is of God; and everyone that loveth is born of God, and knoweth God. He that loveth not knoweth not God; for God is love. . . . And this commandment have we from him, That he who loveth God love his brother also" (I John 4:7-8, 21).

Confess Him before men.

"Whosoever therefore shall confess me before men, him will I confess also before my Father which is in heaven" (Matthew 10:32).

Confess that He is the Son of God.

"Whosoever shall confess that Jesus is the Son of God, God dwelleth in him, and he in God" (I John 4:15).

Some say, "Lord, Lord," but don't do His will.

"Not everyone that saith unto me, Lord, Lord, shall enter into the kingdom of heaven; but he that doeth the will of my Father which is in heaven" (Matthew 7:21). "He that saith, I know him, and keepeth not his commandments, is a liar, and the truth is not in him" (I John 2:4).

13

The Holy Spirit And God's Power Gifts

Wherefore I give you to understand, that no man speaking by the Spirit of God calleth Jesus accursed: and that no man can say that Jesus is Lord, but by the Holy Ghost. Now there are diversities of gifts but the same Spirit . . . But the manifestations of the Spirit is given to every man to profit withal. I Corinthians 12:3-4, 7

THE HOLY SPIRIT MAKETH INTERCESSION—

"Likewise the Spirit also helpeth our infirmities: for we know not what we should pray for as we ought: but the Spirit itself maketh intercession for the saints according to the will of God" (Romans 8:26).

You can believe anything that you want to and I will agree with anything you say you want to believe, as long as what I am agreeing to is for you and not for me! If you say you are something, I'll reply, "Amen, you are something!"

You are only going to have to be around me for the time that you spend reading this book, but you are going to be around you for 24 hours a day, 365 days a year! Remember this, "For as he thinketh in his heart, so is he . . . (Proverbs 23:7).

As for me, I rejoice that the Lord dwells in my heart. That He sent the Holy Spirit to dwell in my heart and life so that I would know that He will never leave me nor forsake me. That I would know that, ". . . lo, I am with you alway, even unto the end of the world" (Matthew 28:20).

This may be the last time I will ever be able to witness to you. Therefore, through words written down on paper, I am going to speak bluntly and "get it all out."

The Lord not only sent the Holy Spirit to me as evidence that He is with me and to reveal Christ unto me, and to reveal *me unto me*, but He also blessed me with His gift of a prayer language which we call "speaking in tongues."

Now, if you don't believe in "speaking in tongues," know this: I Corinthians, 12th chapter, tells us that we receive one Holy Spirit with nine manifestations. Therefore, if you don't believe in "tongues," you don't believe in healing, you don't believe in the miracles, you don't believe in discernment, you don't believe in prophecy. You have to believe it all, Reader, or you don't believe in any of it. The gifts are all listed with commas, not periods, after each one of the gifts. So I say to you, seek the fullness of the Holy Spirit and take what you get, because whatever He gives you is for your good and His glory, and He will bless you with it.

The "prayer language" is given to you as your *secret code. Your secret pipe-line to God.* It is a code that the devil cannot interpret. He cannot understand. It is the biblical evidence of the baptism in the Holy Spirit. It is the accompanying sign. However, it is the Giver of the tongues who is to be magnified. And I magnify above all Him whom the Holy Spirit has come to reveal to us — THE LORD JESUS CHRIST. It is He who sent the Holy Spirit and I rejoice that He makes no difference between us today and those in the beginning.

Sometimes the Holy Spirit gives an interpretation for the tongues. Paul said, ". . . I will pray with the spirit, and I will pray with the understanding also: I will sing with the spirit, and I will sing with the understanding also" (I Corinthians 14:15).

My "understanding," is this: "Lord bless them, keep them, heal them, save them, meet their every need." I understand what I am praying. But, if I pray for you in the spirit, I may not understand. However, Romans 8:26 tells us, "Likewise the spirit also helpeth our infirmities: for we know not what we should pray for as we ought: but the Spirit itself maketh intercession for us with groanings which cannot be uttered." And we read in the 27th verse, "And he that searcheth the hearts knoweth what is the mind of the Spirit, because he maketh intercession for the saints according to the will of God."

Who are the saints the Apostle Paul is referring to?

Not the saints who are over on the other side, but those saints who are here on this earth, walking through the doors that the Lord opens and closes as He reveals His will.

Among the Charismatic people today, a tremendous emphasis has been placed on the gifts of the Holy Spirit. The

Lord knows that in my heart, I would not minimize or take away the importance of the gifts of the Holy Spirit, but I believe that there is something far more important than the gifts in a believer's life, and that is the fruit of the spirit. If you have a Word of knowledge for someone, or a word of prophecy, but you fail to have a word of kindness, or a word of gentleness, or a word of understanding, or tenderness for someone; then you become as sounding brass, and a tinkling cymbal. (I Corinthians 13:1)

You can have the gifts of the Holy Spirit without the fruit, but it is impossible to have the fruit of the Holy Spirit without the gifts. I believe that if God's people will seek for the fruit of the Spirit of the Lord to be manifested in their lives, then, whenever the ministry calls for it, the gifts will be in operation.

"But the fruit of the Spirit is love, joy, peace, long-suffering, gentleness, goodness, faith" (Galatians 5:22). You may not drink, you may not smoke, you may not gamble, you may not carouse and "rev" around, but that "don't make you very hot!" unless you have the fruit of the Spirit dwelling within your heart. There may be many things that you or I don't do, but the world is looking at what we are doing. They aren't interested in how much we speak in tongues, they aren't interested in how much you or I prophesy, they aren't interested in how much we can shout and laugh and clap our hands.

They are interested in one thing — how we treat them. How we treat our fellowmen. Therefore, we should be treating them as Jesus treated us.

Do you want to know something?

You will never be able to do to me what I've done to Christ. I haven't always known what I know, and what I think I know about the Lord. I have a thought in a book of poems entitled "True Knowledge." It reads:

> "True knowledge is knowing that,
> that which you know is nothing
> compared to what there is to
> know about what you know."*

I think a person could title it "True Wisdom." True wisdom is knowing that that which you know is nothing compared to what there is to know about what you know! I used to think that I knew so much about so many things, but the Lord has let me see that even with what I feel I know the most about, there is so much more for me to know about that which I know about, that I am ignorant in my knowledge!

For the above reason, it makes it easy for me to stand in front of a group of people and speak, because I know that everyone else is just as ignorant as I am! But, I am going to learn from you and you are going to learn from me. We are going to learn together, growing in the knowledge of our Lord and Saviour, Jesus Christ. It is only when I know that I can learn from you (and I depend upon your knowledge to teach me) that I am going to endure a lot of things — your idiosyncrasies, your hang-ups, your prejudices. I am not going to let the hang-ups of people rob me out of a blessing of learning that I know that I can receive from them. I would hope that you won't let my little hang-ups rob you of what you might learn from me!

Yes, you will never be able to do to me what I've done to Christ, but our Bible tells us, "And above all things have fervent charity (love) among yourselves: for charity (love) shall cover the multitude of sins" (I Peter 4:8). In His perfect love, Christ gave gifts unto me when He ascended up on high. "Wherefore he saith, When he ascended up on high, he led captivity captive, and gave gifts unto men" (Ephesians 4:8). Then, Paul tells us, "But the manifestation of the Spirit is given to every man to profit withal" (I Corinthians 12:7). So, He gives us the gift of a prayer language, He gives us interpretation, He gives us prophecy. Then, we see the power gifts in operation, which are faith, healing, and miracles.

If faith will cause you to get out of your office, your home, your study, your seat (wherever you might be sitting or the place you may be standing), and go to the altar of God, the faith of the believers there will take them from where they are to pray for you — and if two will agree on earth as touching any thing that they shall ask, it shall be done for them of my Father which is in heaven. (Matthew 18:19)

The Bible tells us that Jesus is on the right hand of the Father making intercession (for whom?) for you and me. ". . . It is Christ that died, yea rather, that is risen again, who is even at the right hand of God, who also maketh intercession for us" (Romans 8:34). If two agree, (you agree and

I agree; we agree) there is no way you can lose in exercising your faith and asking the Father for that which you need.

Every one of your needs can be met by the power of the Spirit of God. Do you know how simple it is? All I need to do is ask someone for a dollar bill. I would keep asking and someone would give me a dollar. It wouldn't cost me a thing. Isn't that nice? It wouldn't cost me a thing! Then, all I would have to do is ask who needed a dollar. You would tell me you needed a dollar and come to me to get it. My friend gave me the dollar because we are friends. He won't ask me what I plan to do with the dollar. He may not even like the person I choose to give the money to! But I know he likes me. So he doesn't care whether he likes you or not, that has nothing to do with it.

You see, you may think that the Father doesn't even like you, but He is going to do it for you — not on your merit but because He is my friend. Jesus is a friend that sticketh closer than a brother. (Proverbs 18:24) He says anyone who's got faith enough to come and get the blessing He will give it to him!

What I am telling you, my friend, is that if you are unsaved the Father will save you; if you are sick in body, soul, or spirit, the Lord will heal you. I say to you, if you want to be filled with the Holy Spirit the Lord will fill you; if you are having financial problems the Lord will help you meet that need. I am telling you that my friend is going to take care of us, but all you have to do is take the first step in faith and receive. You know what your need is. The Lord knows what your need is, and since He is the one who is going to meet your need, it doesn't matter if anyone else knows. If you reach out and accept what the Father is offering to you, you have nothing to lose and everything to gain. "But as it is written, Eye hath not seen, nor ear heard, neither have entered into the heart of man, the things which God hath prepared for them that love him. But God hath revealed them unto us by his Spirit: for the Spirit searcheth all things, yea, the deep things of God" (I Corinthians 2:9-10).

GOD REVEALS HIMSELF UNTO US.

14

What Seest Thou?

The Word of the Lord came to me saying, "Bill Gebrosky, what seest thou?"

I ask you, also, "What do you see?" Reader, what seest thou? Pastor, what seest thou? Husband, what seest thou? Wife, what seest thou? Young people, what seest thou?

What seest thou when you are sitting as part of a congregation, in a fellowship meeting of any kind where Christians are gathered, week after week, month after month? What do you see — sitting where you are?

Do you see a group of men and/or women who are concerned about the kingdom of God? Or, do you see a group of people who are concerned about the kingdom of man? Do you see a group of people who love you, who have been and are concerned about you? Do you see people who want to minister unto your needs?

WHAT DO YOU SEE?

When the Lord spoke of this to me, I looked out over the audience where I was speaking and the Lord said, "Bill, what seest thou?"

When I look at a congregation, what kind of group do I see? Do I see a group of people who keep coming out to meetings because they are hungering and thirsting after the things of God?

There are many different denominations. There are the Catholic, the Baptist, the Lutheran, the Church of Christ; there are many different denominations, but there are only two groups of people in the world today — those going to heaven and those going to hell! Belonging to a church makes you and me about as much a Christian as a piano makes us a musician. We can get our name on every church roll in town, but unless our name is written in the Lamb's book of life, we are lost. (Revelation 21:27) We must know our Lord and Saviour, Jesus Christ, personally. It must be something more than just believing in the doctrine of Christianity and being members of a church. The Father knows all there is to know about us. Even the very hairs on our head are all numbered. (Matthew 10:30) Therefore, we need to come to know Jesus Christ as our Lord and Saviour, who already knows us, and walk day by day with a new revelation of the love that Christ has for each one of us.

If you are a pastor, I ask you: "When you step into your pulpit, what do you see when you look into the faces of your congregation?" How long have you been pastoring there? How long has the Lord called you to lead the sheep? As you look over the congregation, do you see a group of people who are well-fed, who are nurtured? Who are raised in the fear and admonition of the Lord? Who have been taught through your instruction? People who are happy in their relationship to Christ? What seest thou when you look at them, Pastor?

Congregation, I ask you: "When you go to your churches and look at your priest, your preacher, or your pastor, what do you see? Do you see a man who is going to get up there and tell you about the Watergate, about this social, and about that "going-on," about the things printed in your newspapers or broadcast over television? Or, do you see a man who stands up there and tells you that there is a city whose builder and maker is God? That there is a God who loves you? That there is a Christ who is concerned about you? That there is a Spirit of the Lord who dwells in the land today to nurture us, to encourage us, to strengthen us, to heal us, and to bless us?

I believe that on Sunday morning there are a lot of ministers who step behind the pulpit and the only thing that the people get from that pulpit is what is going on in the CIA, what is going on in the Middle East, what's happening on the political scene. The congregation hears nothing about Jesus because the man who is supposed to be ministering the gospel does not know Him.

But, praise the Lord, there are a lot of ministers who do know Jesus as their personal Saviour. They are preaching the gospel of Jesus Christ.

I believe that in the Catholic church there are a lot of priests who will get up on Sunday morning or Saturday night, and when they read their homily, all the people will receive is a letter from the Bishop. But I know personally many priests, and sisters, and laity, who do know Jesus as their Saviour.

There are men in all denominations who do know Jesus as their Saviour and there are many men in all denominations who don't. But, know this — you and I must have a personal relationship with Christ.

Husbands, when you look at your wives, what do you really see? When you look at her do you see a woman who is your helpmate? A woman who loves the Lord and loves you because of her love for the Lord?

Woman, look at your husband, "what seest thou?" Do you see a man who is concerned about your welfare, about your kindness, your gentleness, your tenderness, and your understanding? What seest thou?

Parents, I ask you: when you look at your children, what do you really see? Do you see kids who look at their parents with love, respect and admiration? Do you see kids who have been raised in the fear and admonition of the Lord? What do you see?

Young people, what seest thou? When you look at your parents, what do you really see? Do you see two people who are striving to serve the Lord? Striving to show to you the love that God has shown to them? What seest thou?

And, Reader, what seest thou when you and I look in the face of the Lord? What do you and I see when we lift our voices and sing songs of praise and adoration? What do we see when we look into the Scriptures and see Him? What does He see when He looks at you and me?

"Lord," I ask, "what seest thou when you look at Bill Gebrosky? When you look at my next door neighbor, my friend across town or across the country?"

When He looks at you, what kind of person does He see?

In the first chapter of John, the Apostle was asked, "Who art thou? What sayest thou of thyself?"

You and I can answer the question of "what seest thou?" when we look at another person, but can that person answer the same question when he looks at us — or must he ask, "Who art thou?"

If you and I had the opportunity to stand and give a word of witness and testimony right now, would you say, "Lord, this is what you see in me. This is what I am going to stand and proclaim, Lord, that this is what you see."

You are not supposed to point your finger at yourself; that is not having humility. I tell you, "humility in the eyes of ability is hypocrisy." (John 3:27; Matthew 25:14-30;

I Peter 4:10) There are so many people under the guise of humility who have become nothing but hypocrites. God has given us an ability. He did not make us robots or puppets on a string. He said, "I have given you a heart to love me; I have given you a Saviour to meet your every need in your spirit, soul, and body." (I Chronicles 28:9; I Corinthians 2:16; Deuteronomy 6:5; Jeremiah 24:7; I John 4:14; Philippians 4:19)

Lord, let me stand and tell you what I think you see when you look at me. You see that I have failed many times. I have been weak in a lot of situations. I have had many heartaches and sorrows. On some occasions, I have turned my back on the things that I have known that you wanted me to do. But, I know that through all of this, Lord, that when you look at me, you look at a child who is nothing but a child. You look at a person who is many years old in the Lord, one who recognizes that he has faults, who knows that he makes mistakes. But I know one thing for certain, You love me. You loved me when I first accepted you as my Lord and Saviour, and how much more You must love me today.

What seest thou, Lord, when you look at these needy people? We didn't ask for all the situations of life. We didn't ask you for a world that is not at peace. We didn't ask you for all the sickness that is in this life. So, we look to you today, Lord, asking you to make us well, to speak peace to our troubled heart and soul as you spoke peace to the storm.

"What sayest thou of thyself, John?" the Lord asked the Apostle. "Just who art thou? and then, when you know who you are, what do you see? Just what thinkest thou?" What do you think about, what do you dwell upon? What do you meditate upon? You and I know what we think about. We know what is uppermost in our minds and our spirits. We know what we concern ourselves with. We know that many times we have run to and fro trying to find the answer to our problems when our answer has only been a prayer away.

Our answer has been as close as a bended knee, our voice crying out, "Lord, here I am, just as I am." And the Lord cuddles us up in His arms and with tender, loving care whispers in our ear, "Child, I do love you. I do want you. I do need you. I am concerned about you." And He admonishes us from His wisdom, "Think upon those things which are pure, upon those things which are good, upon those things which are honest." (Philippians 4:8)

It is humanly impossible to think about two things at the same time. If you are down in the dumps, it is because you want to think you are down in the dumps.

Now, I am not talking about a Christian Science doctrine.

There was a guy who went up to a man and said, "You know, my brother is sick."

"Look," the man replied, "you go back and tell your brother that he only thinks he is sick. He is not really sick."

So, this fellow went back and reported to his brother, "You are not sick, you just think you are."

Three weeks later, the man saw this guy again and asked him, "Hey, how is your brother?"

"You know, he thinks he is dead," he replied.

If we think in the negative vein of life, if we dwell upon the heartaches and sorrows, if we dwell upon the mistakes, then we will always be down in the dumps. If, however, we will lift our eyes toward heaven and realize that we are in the boat with Christ, no matter how deep the water, as long as we are in the boat, the deeper the water, the closer to heaven we rise. So, let it rain, let it pour! I will praise God forevermore, as I lift my heart and my hands to Him! I am in the boat with Him!

Reader, if He can sleep while He is in the boat, there is no sense of my getting excited. He said to the disciples, "Let us get in the boat and go over." Let us go over to the other side of the sea, and they launched forth. I see in this Scripture a hidden meaning. There can't be too much importance in going over to the other side of the sea, so the author must be talking about something else. I feel that He is saying, "Get into the boat with me and when you pass from the body into the life in my presence; then, you will know what it is all about." In other words, "Let us be so busy going over that we do not have time to go under." I ask you, "What thinkest thou?"

The Lord God called unto Adam and said, "Where art thou?" (Genesis 3:9) Adam heard the Lord walking in the garden in the cool of the day, and he ran to hide himself from the presence of God.

I ask you, where are you right now? Where are you in your relationship with Christ? Where are you in your relationships, one with the other? Just where are you? Adam said, "I heard your voice and I was afraid. I am over here, hiding in the bushes."

When the Lord comes to reveal Himself to you, where will you be hiding? Is there anything you are hiding behind today? You know that Adam took fig leaves and tried to cover his nakedness, but God who loved Adam and Eve wanted to walk with them, wanted fellowship with them. Even though they sinned, God did not stop loving them. Instead, He said to Adam and his wife, Eve, also, "I know that I can't walk with you now in your nakedness because your innocence is gone. You know good and evil. But, Adam, you can't cover your nakedness. Let me cover it for you." The Lord God made coats of skins and clothed them. (Genesis 3:21)

One day, long ago, the Lord said to me, "Bill Gebrosky, I'd love to walk with you, but I can't walk with you in your sin. Let me cover you with something."

"What can you cover me with, Lord?" I asked.

"I want to cover you with the blood of Jesus Christ."

When the Father looks at me and He looks at you (if you are a Christian), He no longer sees our sins, He sees what we are covered with, which is the blood of Christ.

I didn't see any blood go over me. I felt no blood go over me, but I just know that when it happened on October 3, 1954, I was reborn into the family of God.

The Lord asks us, "What seest thou? What thinkest thou? What sayest thou of thyself?' and "Where art thou?" There is one more question that He asks. When Elijah was in the cave, the Lord said, "What art thou doing in this place?" (I Kings 19:9)

I ask you, "What are you doing in the place where you are? What are you doing in life? What does life hold for you? What do you get out of life?"

My friend, you get everything you invest. If you are suffering heartache and sorrow, it may be because you have invested in heartache and sorrow. If you feel that nobody loves you, it may be because you haven't loved anybody. If you feel that you are not understood, it may be because you are not understanding. If you feel nobody cares, it might be because you do not care. If you say, "Everybody's talking about me," could it be because you are talking about everybody else? Whatsoever ye sow, you will surely reap. (Galatians 6:7) He also said that He will bless them that bless you. Go around being a blessing to people and the Lord will be a blessing to you. But He also said that He will curse them that curse you. (Genesis 12:3)

One final question I ask of you, "Where are you going?" I will tell you a place you are going, if Jesus tarries, you are going right out there to the "body locker." There is going to come a time when an undertaker is going to have a little smile on his face as he reads your insurance policy, a smile while he is pumping that embalming fluid in your veins. ... .

There was a rich man who died in Wichita. I attended his funeral. Sitting in front of me were two elderly ladies. The one turned and whispered loudly to the other, "I wonder how much he left?"

Leaning over the back of the seat, I said, "I think he left it all!"

I ask you, friend, where art thou going? You cannot escape the grave if Jesus tarries. There are many people buried every day. I know that.

". . . truly as the Lord liveth, there is but a step between me and death" (I Samuel 20:3d).

If you do not know Christ as your personal Saviour — why don't you invite Him into your life at this very moment.

For all of those who are following after Christ — "you too can be a happy Christian, even tho' you're spirit filled." If you are at Peace with God, with yourself and with your fellow man.—

God Bless you all. I love you very much.

BILL GEBROSKY
SIX SCRIPTURE STEPS TO SALVATION**

1 Acknowledge: "For all have sinned and come short of the glory of God" (Romans 3:23). "God be merciful to me a sinner" (Luke 18:13). You must acknowledge in the light of God's Word that you are a sinner.

2 Repent: "Except ye repent, ye shall all likewise perish" (Luke 13:3). "Repent ye therefore, and be converted, that your sins may be blotted out" (Acts 3:19). You must see the awfulness of sin and then repent of it.

3 Confess: "If we confess our sins, he is faithful and just to forgive us our sins, and to cleanse us from all unrighteousness" (I John 1:9). "With the mouth confession is made unto salvation" (Romans 10:10). The Lord awaits your admission of guilt.

4 Forsake: "Let the wicked forsake his way, and the unrighteous man his thoughts: and let him return unto the Lord . . . for he will abundantly pardon" (Isaiah 55:7). Sorrow for sin is not enough in itself. We must want to be done with it once and for all.

5 Believe: "For God so loved the world, that he gave his only begotten Son, that whosoever believeth in him should not perish, but have everlasting life" (John 3:16). "If thou shalt confess with thy mouth the Lord Jesus, and shalt believe in thine heart that God hath raised Him from the dead, thou shalt be saved" (Romans 10:9). "He that believeth and is baptized shall be saved; but he that believeth not shall be damned" (Mark 16:16). Believe in the finished work of Christ on the cross.

6 Receive: "He came unto his own, and his own received him not. But as many as received him, to them gave he power to become the sons of God, even to them that believe on his name" (John 1:11-12). Christ must be received personally into the heart by faith, if the experience of the New Birth is to be yours.

A SINNER'S PRAYER FOR RECEIVING THE SAVING KNOWLEDGE OF JESUS CHRIST***

"I am convinced by God's Word that I am a lost sinner. I believe that Jesus Christ died for sinners and shed His blood to put away my sins. I NOW RECEIVE HIM as my PERSONAL LORD AND SAVIOUR and will by His help confess Him before men." Amen and Amen.

When you have made this greatest of all decisions, please let us know about it so that we may rejoice together.

Name .... Address ....

City/State/Zip ....

Mail to: Bill Gebrosky Evangelistic Association of Kansas

Box 2015, Wichita, Kansas 67201

"SEND US YOUR PRAYER REQUESTS."

More delightful poetry
by Bill Gebrosky
is available in:

Inspirational Poetry For Daily Living $1.25

Dear Father Help Me $1.25

HARRISON HOUSE
P.O. Box 35035
Tulsa, Okla. 74135